DOMENICO CARDINAL TARDINI

MEMORIES

OF

PIUS XII

Translated by
ROSEMARY GOLDIE

THE NEWMAN PRESS
Westminster, Maryland - 1961

First published in English, 1961

Library of Congress Catalog Card Number: 60-53377

Printed in Italy

CONTENTS

MILD AND HEROIC

6

We are happy to publish
by gracious permission
of HIS HOLINESS JOHN XXIII
the Eulogy of Pope Pius XII
which He pronounced in Venice
in St. Mark's Patriarchal Basilica
on October 11th, 1958

Bene omnia fecit: et surdos fecit audire et mutos loqui
(Mark 7, 36 *f.*).

On all occasions, here in St. Mark's Basilica, my words seek inspiration from our patron, the Evangelist. This funeral rite celebrated to honour and to pray for the blessed soul of our glorious Pontiff, Pius XII, who has passed during these days to the heavenly regions, could not find a better context than the testimony which St. Mark—himself, *Filius et interpres Petri*—gathered for us from the lips of the crowd, moved to ecstasy by Jesus' miracles. It was of no avail to try to impose silence upon their wonderment: *magis plus praedicabant, eo amplius admirabantur, dicentes: bene omnia fecit: et surdos fecit audire et mutos loqui* (Mark 7, 36 f.).

9

For nearly twenty years this voice of Pius XII, Servant of the Servants of God, of the Angelic Pastor, was heard each day anew within the frontiers of his fatherland, proclaiming good doctrine, admonishing, encouraging individual souls and countless multitudes to well-doing. Oftentimes, these frontiers were crossed, as in the days of Jesus, beyond Tyre, towards the sea of Galilee, through the Decapolis, to the furthest and most distant parts.

It was the miracles that spoke in the days of Jesus: with Pius XII, it was his voice that became ever more operative and more penetrating, until it became transformed into a world-wide acclamation.

Your Patriarch, my beloved people, still remembers how, years ago, at the end of January, 1922, he pronounced, in his accustomed simple language, a funeral discourse in honour of Pope Benedict XV. It was in the parish church of Castelgandolfo, next to the papal villa, then silent and deserted, and the theme was the same quotation from St. Mark: *bene omnia fecit.*

Seven blood-stained years of war had sufficed

for the glory of Benedict XV, who was tiny in stature, but so great in mind and heart. It was from him, one day, on May 13th, 1917, that, with the episcopal anointing, the divine virtue had flowed which was to place the steps of the young prelate, Eugenio Pacelli, on the road leading to the heights of the supreme priesthood.

But, what must we say of him, of Pope Pius XII, after almost four lustrums, which for him, too, were years of war, rather than of peace? What must we say of him who has made the earth vibrate with his teaching, re-echo with his words, adding to the resonance of his voice the marvels of a pastoral activity which twenty volumes can not contain?

Yesterday afternoon, watching on direct or re-corded television the transfer of the Pope's remains from Castelgandolfo to the Lateran and to St. Peter's in the Vatican, it occured to me to wonder whether the triumphal progress of an ancient Roman Emperor towards the Capitol could have equal-led—not as a display of military power, but in

11

impressive dignity, in spiritual majesty and depth of feeling—the magnitude of this spectacle which touched so many hearts. Once again there came back to my mind the words of our great Lombard writer: " So strong is charity! Among the varied and solemn memories of a general disaster, charity can give pride of place to the memory of one man, because it has inspired this man to feelings and actions more memorable still than the evils which have befallen; it imprints on men's minds, as it were, a recapitulation of all these ills, because in all of them its urging has made of him a guide, a succour, an example, a willing victim; what is a calamity for all, it can make, as it were, for this man, into an exploit; appoint it, for him, as a conquest or a discovery."

It is the surpassing charity of his actions over a period of more than eighty years that merits for him the tribute with which the crowds hailed the passage of Jesus of Nazareth. *Bene omnia fecit.* He has done all things well.

And the tribute is complete when we single

12

out two great victories characteristic of Pius XII's pontificate: by the constant flow of his lofty and divine teaching, he opened the ears of the deaf and restored their speech to the dumb: he made the silent to speak.

Oh! the *magisterium* of Pius XII! The comments which have been and continue to be aroused by the news of his death are unanimous, above all, as to the importance, the varied and harmonious beauty, the richness of the teaching of this great master of the faith. That teaching, rivalling the splendours of the Fathers and Doctors of the ancient Church, has contrived to adapt itself to the most modern conditions, making its own of modern thought while respecting the doctrinal inheritance of former generations. At the same time, it has increased the sacred heritage for the benefit of human and Christian civilization, for the progress of nations, establishing those prerequisites for the nations' upward course which—it has been well written—" come from religion, from Christianity, from Catholicism, from that army

13

drawn up for a bloodless and holy combat, which is the Church, from that guiding summit, which is Peter's pontificate."

Of Pius XII, history will tell how happily his teaching, unprecedented in its intensity, was conceived; how timely, effective, and indispensable it was for this age in which—be it noted—society has left to the Church alone the freedom of speech necessary for one who would not walk in darkness and lose sight of the pole-star.

When speaking to upright and sincere persons, I have often had occasion to compare the Church's sacred *magisterium*, characteristic of the Holy Father, Pius XII, to the public fountain placed at the centre of an inhabited area, whether town or village. Its teaching extends to the various sectors of life according to the fluctuations of human relationships, or as awkward circumstances arise or are unexpectedly encountered. All citizens have access to the public fountain and can derive advantage and benefit from it according to the varying demands of the vicissitudes of human life.

This is not the place to enter more deeply into this tribute to his great dignity as a universal teacher which completes in an extraordinary way the exceptional merits of Pius XII. It is the light of the charity of Christ Our Lord shining upon the visage of His Vicar on earth, intent on glorifying—in theological, ascetical, mystical, apostolic, and social works—the Kingdom of Christ, a kingdom of truth and grace, of justice, love, and peace.

This deposit of the most sacred truths thrown into clear relief, this zeal in speaking of them, in illustrating them day by day for the spiritual food of souls, was one of the brightest rays of Pius XII's spiritual *magisterium*.

For his part, always and in every circumstance, he worked the miracle, placing his fingers upon men's ears crying *ephphetha* (Mark 7, 34).

Did the deaf to whom he spoke respond, or do they respond by perfect hearing? This is the secret of grace. This is the extraordinary merit of the pontiff, in his first anointing as divine teacher.

In the case of souls, it is already a great achievement to have left no excuse for hardened rejection of known truth. *Bene omnia fecit: surdos fecit audire!*—a great title to honour and merit.

The other aspect of Pius XII's pontificate and of his illustrious merits, the *mutos loqui*, is to be seen in the consoling spectacle of these days, which tempers and allays our grief now that the Common Father has left us for the heavenly regions.

Anxieties and reasons for sadness have never been wanting in God's Church. At times, even what can be an occasion for quiet reflection on the truths of religion and excite to reverent acts of filial piety, becomes, on the contrary, a cause of regret and even of dreadful suffering.

When we go back in memory to the deaths of the great pontiffs of recent times, painful reminders are not wanting.

An illustrious and holy Pope of the last century was the Servant of God, Pius IX, of whom it was written that no Pope was ever more loved and more hated on this earth: and I remember the profit and edification I derived in my adolescence and youth from reading the poignant story of his life and pontificate. The memory, however, is still present—it brings a blush of shame for the perpetrators of the diabolical undertaking, and horror to every decent man—of how the attempt was made to throw his sacred bones into the Tiber when they were being transferred from the cemetery of the Campo Verano to St. Lawrence's Basilica, where the Catholics of Europe had prepared a stately tomb, still visited with respect and veneration.

In 1903, I had only just taken Major Orders, when on July 20th, at the age of ninety-three, Pope Leo XIII, passed away after a pontificate of twenty five years. The funeral ceremonies were, indeed, of the greatest solemnity, but exclusively of an official and ecclesiastical character and confined to St. Peter's Basilica. The Rome of civic and political life remained silent and contemptuous. The next Popes: St. Pius X, Benedict XV, and Pius XI, were attended in death, to be sure, with deep reverence, and the religious solemnities were liturgically perfect and in pontifical style. But there were no signs of unusual emotion.

With our Holy Father, Pius XII, on the contrary—it is most consoling to admit—we are clearly witnessing the opening up of new horizons, and of something which mysteriously reveals a gradual improvement in relations between the civil order and the religious and social order: a stronger inclination to reverence for the sacred; a readiness—even though we belong to different schools of thought in political, economic, and sociological matters—to look one another in the eyes with the desire for more harmonious relations.

It would seem that, by rising to such heights, this Pope, whose name will go down among the greatest and most popular of modern history, has won greater respect for all that the Head of the Catholic Church signifies and recapitulates in his person; and this can only be to the good.

And so we not only have the fingers of the Divine Wonder-worker placed upon the ear of the deaf man with the words " be opened ", but even the saliva of Jesus touching the lips once sealed and unlocking them to the living resonance of speech.

The achievement of the *Bene omnia fecit* is thus complete: *et fecit mutos loqui.*

At this point, however, a wave of sadness passes over my spirit. The whole world has been moved by the Pope's death, and is gathered on the heights of Mount Olivet, like the disciples for the last farewell, as though to accompany him with eyes and heart as he rises towards Heaven.

But there is one part of the world where vast sections of the children of the Catholic Church are cut off from public display in our universal grief.

The Holy Father called these sections the " Church of Silence."

My beloved people and brethren! You understand my meaning. To think of the " Church of Silence " while we are gathered around the Pope who, though dead, is yet living and who so often voiced its lamentations is like praying with him to the heavenly Father to put an end to this trial;

to the trial of these lips, which remain half-closed while hearts are bursting with groans of anguish under the weight and enslavement of a severe persecution, organized with a diabolical audacity unrivalled by anything man has attempted up to the present time.

O Holy Father, as you pass through the ethereal regions toward the peace of God, instructed by your example we invite you to lend our prayer the strength of your own: *Exurge Domine, adjuva nos, et libera nos propter nomen tuum.*

One more word.

As we listen to the voices rising from the earth, we have the feeling that the departure of our most holy Pontiff and Father has turned into an impressive world-wide triumph for his name and person. Raised to the heavenly regions, he would even seem to be looking upon us and repeating the words which I think can be attributed to St. Gregory the Great: *Meus honor et honor universalis Ecclesiae; est fratrum meorum solidus vigor:* my honour, the honour you pay to me, is the honour of the universal Church; for you, my children, it is a source of robust spiritual vigour. From the bottom of my heart I wish that it may be so indeed.

Meanwhile, O blessed and holy Father, accept the boundless gratitude which the whole Catholic world owes to you: the gratitude which not Catholics alone, but all those—even though they may not share in Catholic unity—who bear upon their brow the name of Christ, all those who are united by a feeling of human brotherhood, voice in this moving plebiscite of grief, admiration, and love.

The last words you dictated in your testament were a prayer for mercy, a cry of fatherhood and brotherhood, a plea for pardon.

Of this pardon we all stand in need.

Behold, our arms are outstretched; and with the saints of God we raise you up in sight of the Most High.

You were the Angelic Pastor and you led us to the pastures of eternal life; you were the defender of our fatherland in its most tragic hours; be so yet again, O Pope Pius, be ever so, O flower,

O glory of the Italian people: be ever so, and bless our homes, our families, our priests, the poor, the suffering, the children. Bless Venice (*whose horizons today reach out, as far as our prayer, to the whole of Christendom*), Venice, whose loyal ranks were always close about your apostolic throne and which will never cease to honour your memory, as you will rejoice her always with your love and heavenly protection.

O Holy Father, never to be forgotten: *sit super nos semper benedictio tua. Amen.*

COMMEMORATION OF H. H. PIUS XII
ON THE FIRST ANNIVERSARY
OF HIS DEATH

On Tuesday, October 20th, 1959, in the hall of the Benedictions at the Vatican, in presence of the august Pontiff, John XXIII, gloriously reigning, of the Sacred College of Cardinals, of the diplomatic corps and of a select audience of prelates and ecclesiastical and lay personalities, H. E. Domenico Cardinal Tardini, Secretary of State of His Holiness, recalled the figure and the works of the great Pontiff, Pius XII.

Most Holy Father,

Last year, two days after the death of Pius XII, you pronounced his panegyric in St. Mark's Basilica.

In your commemoration—which breathes deep-felt emotion and affection—you called the Great Pontiff: The Pope who, though dead, is yet living.

Yes, Pius XII is still living: living in the glory to which Our Lord has called him; living in the affectionate memory of mankind; living, above all, in those who had, for long years, the grace of being close to him.

On that occasion, Most Holy Father, you commented on the words of the Palestinian crowds, which St. Mark reports in his Gospel: Bene omnia fecit: et surdos fecit audire et mutos loqui (Mark 7, 36 f.).

Pius XII did all things: all that was his duty, all that lay in his power; and all things well.

Permit me now, Most Holy Father, to apply to myself the words which follow in the Gospel—those which refer to the deaf and to the dumb.

I was not deaf, for my ear was at all times strained

25

for the teachings of Pius XII, listening to them, even if I was not always equally ready to put them into practice.

But dumb, I was dumb, for it was my duty then to labour and be silent.

Today the dumb man will speak and, as Your Holiness has graciously provided, he will speak in your august presence.

Even if the dumb man should become too loquacious, his words, though springing from his heart, will still be inadequate to express the merits and the greatness of the immortal Pontiff.

In this hour when the memory of the past fills us with serene sadness, allow me, Most Holy Father, at least to mention a consoling reality of the present.

I do not want to wound your modesty; it would be ungenerous. I do not want to flatter your sacred Person; it would be unseemly.

But it is a fact that, one year after the passing of Pius XII, you, most Holy Father, have already contrived to win the sympathy, the esteem, and the tender affection of the whole world.

These are the wondrous secrets of God's Providence, sending to His Church worthy and zealous pastors.

Popes die, the Pope does not die.

" Coronam de spinis imposuerunt capiti eius "

(John 19, 2)

March 12th, 1956 was the Seventeenth Anniversay of
the Coronation of His Holiness Pius XII.

That day, at the close of my usual audience, as I
knelt before him to receive his almost daily blessing, I
respectfully offered my wishes for the anniversary.

The Pope replied with a faint smile: a smile of min-
gled sadness and resignation. He remained a few moments in silence, gazing straight before him, as though
trying to see something afar off, to recall, as it were, a
now distant past. Then his eyes, filled with tears, were
lowered towards me as, clasping my hand in a kindly
gesture, he murmured with deep emotion in moving
tones: " Dear Monsignor, a crown of thorns! "

That day's scene will ever remain stamped on my
memory and on my heart. But I recall it more vividly,

27

and the emotion revives with fresh intensity and new tenderness as I prepare to commemorate the great figure of the immortal Pontiff.

Towards the heights

With him, the Lord had been lavish in His gifts: a keen, brilliant, versatile intellect; a prompt and generous will; an amazing memory. To these and many other fine natural qualities, add a fervent piety, boundless charity, absolute devotion to duty, constant and almost unremitting intensity of effort in his work, heroic readiness for renunciation and sacrifice, and you will see how Divine Providence prepared this soul for its noble destiny.

It is not too much to say that Our Lord led His faithful servant, as it were, by the hand.

From the serene intimacy of an exemplary Roman family to the priesthood. Then, while still very young —in February 1901—he was called to the Sacred Congregation for Extraordinary Ecclesiastical Affairs, which Pius XII liked to call the *Dicastery of government*.[1] He remained there until 1917: a long period comprising the last years of Leo XIII, the whole pontificate of St. Pius X, and three years of the first world war, which coincided with the beginning of Benedict XV's pontificate.

As Nuncio in Munich, and later in Berlin, Msgr. Pacelli withnessed the collapse of Germany, then its recovery, and finally, the first symptoms of Nazism.

In December, 1929, Pius XI recalled Msgr. Pacelli to Rome, now as a Cardinal and very soon afterwards as Secretary of State.[2]

And so we find him taking part in the government of the Church alongside another great Pope who entertained such esteem and affection for him that he became his guide and teacher and consciously prepared him—not without divine inspiration—to be his successor on the throne of Peter.[3]

A great Pontiff

When raised to the office of Sovereign Pontiff, Pius XII brought with him an abundance of treasures, stored up during the long years of patient, unceasing toil in posts of confidence and responsibilities of government: treasures of knowledge, of personal observation, of study, of difficulties overcome, of battles fought, of agreements painstakingly negotiated and successfully concluded; in a word, of so many experiences, one more valuable than the other, which are rarely found together in the life of one man.

Our Lord granted Pius XII a long pontificate:—almost twenty years. And, during those years, what a vast range of events! What a terrible period in the history of the world and in the life of the Church! What a mass of responsibilities weighed upon the Pope, and how appalling the volume of work to which, knowingly and willingly, he bent his energies! [4]

Within the context of so many and such tragic vicissitudes, Pius XII appeared, and was, indeed, great.

He was great as a teacher of truth; great as peacemaker between peoples; great as judge of a humanity which seemed to revel in its guilt; great as most tender Father for all his children; great as comforter and benefactor of the suffering; great, above all, as a soul constantly united to Our Lord and striving ever more ardently after divine perfection.

Crown of thorns

In all of these ways, Pius XII merited, before God and before men, a dazzling crown of glory. But, at the same time, as the Pope himself had occasion to say, his was a painful " crown of thorns."

Through each day's—I would almost say, each hour's—suffering, his greatness and his glory came to maturity.

30

He confided his suffering to his intimates, but above all, he confided in Our Lord.

He must have meditated long before the tabernacle on suffering, whose stinging wounds he bore within his heart. As proof and fruit of this sweet converse, we find the ever recurring and re-echoing theme of suffering in the wonderful symphony of his discourses and messages.

In this amazing wealth of texts—from which it would be possible to gather a valuable anthology under the title " Pius XII and Human Suffering "—there is one text which is particularly important because it sums up in a few sentences the whole Catholic teaching on the efficacy of suffering as a sanctifying element in the life of a soul.

A revealing text

The text is contained in a prayer [5] with which, on January 26th, 1946, Pius XII concluded the address he gave in St. Peter's to fifty thousand children.

The Pope compared these " adolescent souls " to " fragile roses, offering to the early morning sun, which floods them with light and warmth, the delicate fragrance and fresh tints of their scarce unfolded petals."

After these opening words, which would be called

poetical, the style and tone of the beautiful prayer change, the accents become grave, the phrases terse and incisive.

The sanctifying power of suffering

" O God of goodness, if, for their own sakes, Thou dost deem well in Thy infinite wisdom not to spare them suffering, if Thou dost see that they need this initiation, this purification, this refining crucible, this test of patience, this light of the spirit, this mark of human solidarity, this touchstone of love, then at least, let the abundance of Thy grace sustain their trustful spirits, strengthen them in danger, lead them safely through the uncertainties of the way."[6]

The chalice of suffering

This short passage which spells out, as it were, the factors of sanctification in human suffering has the perfection of a synthesis and the completeness of an analysis.

Anyone who knew Pius XII well will recognize in these words his profound psychological, moral, and theological understanding, but above all, will catch the tones (I would even say, the lament) of a heart that suffering has severely tried.

For him, too-—to use his own words—suffering was

the *initiation* which set his course and spurred him on along the paths of sanctity; it was the *crucible* which purified and refined his soul; the *light of the spirit* whose indescribable radiance shone at all times through his being.

He accepted and valued suffering as a constant *test of patience*, giving strength and vigour to his virtues, as a *mark of human solidarity*, steeling his heroic will for sacrifice on behalf of his brethren and his children.

Suffering, finally, was the *touchstone* which tested and authenticated his ardent and generous charity towards God and men.

His soul, rich in exquisite and most delicate sensibility, drained, drop by drop, the bitter chalice of suffering.[7] Not only the terrible vicissitudes of the war and the troubled period which followed, heavy with threats and dangers, but, we may say, every one of the manifold forms of his inexhaustible activity cost him fatigue, sacrifice, interior struggles, and almost superhuman effort.

Sublime victory

Sustained by trust in God, he was able, however, to master his inward distress, and he appeared to all serene, often smiling, always graciously kind and approachable.

Was this no more than a misleading outward appearance?

Surely not.

Pius XII always candidly revealed his inward dispositions.

Constantly united to God, he was able to remain calm through the storm, and serene through bitterness; he was concerned, but not troubled; distressed, but not discouraged; the hardest struggles did not change nor diminish the even sweetness of his inward peace.[8]

Pius XII appeared also to be—and was in reality—happy. He took pleasure in lively conversation, and appreciated fine literary phrases, like a humanist of the Renaissance. As a true Roman, he loved and relished wit, and was quick to see the humorous, so often hidden in the inexhaustible variety of human affairs.[9]

When he laughed, with his wide mouth open, his eyes flashing, and his arms raised, he looked—allow me to say so, for I cannot find any other comparison—like a happy child.

This was the " perfect joy," which is also a reward and fruit of suffering.

In a world situation of authentic tragedy, Pius XII was said to be—and was, in fact—the *dominant* figure, while in reality he was at the same time the first *victim*.

Himself the most *afflicted* of all, he was for all the *Comforter*.

He inspired the crowds and carried them away; but his keenest and deepest longing was for study, meditation, and solitude.

An outstanding speaker, he seemed to delight in his polished and vigorous eloquence. And yet, every one of those speeches and messages cost him long-drawn and laborious effort.

Wise in his guidance, how often he pointed out the sure path to others; yet it was not uncommon for him to go through the greatest anguish in seeking out the way for himself.

Mild by temperament, he was naturally inclined to avoid strife. But he could be an intrepid warrior whenever necessary for the safeguard of truth and justice and for the good of souls. Pius XII will thus go down in history as a Pontiff who was a wise reformer and a daring innovator.

This whole complex of contrasts and contradictions

throws light on what I would dare to call the mystery of Pius XII.

Unless we understand all this, it will never be possible to appreciate his outstanding merits, the perfection of his great virtues: a perfection—it is well to point out—which was won by sweat and toil.

Yet another grace was granted to one who remained for many years close to Pius XII: that of witnessing his spiritual ascent, seeing him constantly rise, become purified, refined, mellowed, grow in stature.

At the end, the flame of his charity, having burned up the tiniest fragment of the dross of human frailty, poured out and spread over the earth its flashes of heavenly radiance.

MAN OF PEACE
POPE OF WAR

When, on March 2nd, 1939, Eugenio Pacelli was raised to the office of Sovereign Pontiff, the rumour went round (one of those scraps of gossip which are always around at such moments) that certain of Their Eminences had been rather reluctant from the beginning to give him their votes, in view of the threatening international situation. " Cardinal Pacelli, " they said, " is a *man of peace* and the world today needs a *pope of war*."

Humanly speaking, the judgment was correct.

Eugenio Pacelli was, indeed, a man of peace. The delicacy of his feelings, his innate courtesy, his gentle forebearance inclined him to overcome difficulties by patience and perseverance, avoiding strong words, harsh phrases, abrupt gestures. All of this made him disposed to love, desire, and work for peace.

By this method, combining firmness with courtesy, foreign to heated rivalries and favorable to calm discussion, Eugenio Pacelli, during his mission in Germany, successfully concluded two important concordats: with Bavaria in 1924 and with Prussia in 1929.

Pope of war

And yet, this man, who was peace-loving by temperament, education, and conviction, was to have what might be called a pontificate *of war:* hot or cold, world-wide or local, but always war.

The most peace-loving of men was never again to know a moment's peace.

He accepted his heavy cross from the hand of God. He suffered; he brought relief; he spoke; he acted.

All the sufferings of others found an echo in his sensitive, paternal heart.

To relieve the countless and unspeakable miseries of the war, he gave all that he had and he gave himself wholly. He mobilized the radio and the diplomatic service; he created the Pontifical Relief Commission; he took into his palaces the homeless and those who were in danger—all were saved, if not all grateful—; he fed and saved the population of Rome, which acclaimed him with one voice *Defensor civitatis;* he hastened to St. Lawrence's and St. John Lateran after the bombing; he sought anxiously for news of the missing; he instructed his representatives to visit and take his gifts to the prisoners; he offered the gold demanded by the Nazis for the safety of the Jews; he appealed on behalf of those who were deported and condemned to death. He gave out his own food, multipied his penances, and did not want his apartment to be heated in the severe winter.

Few people know that, at the end of the war, Pius XII was so thin and emaciated that he weighed only 57 kilograms (125 pounds). His height—it will be well to point out—was 1.82 m. (almost 6 ft.).

The doctors were worried. "The Pope has no disease," they said, "but in his present state, even the slightest illness can prove fatal."

In 1948, when the war had been over for three years and he had given up the use of his summer residence at Castelgandolfo for so long, he still did not want to leave Rome. "What will people who are suffering think," he asked, "when they know that the Pope goes off to the country?"

It was only in August that he could be prevailed on to leave.

We have spoken of the sufferings and the active charity of the Father. We must not forget the exhausting labours and the noble task of the *Teacher*.

Placed by God in so exalted a position and drawn spiritually to Himself, animated by the firmest of faith, sustained by unshakable trust, urged on by inexhaustible charity, the Pope considered it his duty to let his voice be heard often.

And his was a voice of truth, justice, love.

That was the beginning of the wonderful series of addresses, letters, messages which was to continue, uninterruptedly, for almost twenty years.

It would not be possible to recall here all the reminders, the admonitions, the teachings, the exhortations which Pius XII addressed to the world. War, peace, the social order, international relations, the family, economic affairs, science, labour: these and so many other themes recur in his impassioned oratory.

He deplored violations of the law (the three famous telegrams of May 10th, 1940 were composed by him personally)[10]; he invited the belligerents to show moderation; he rose up in defence of the unarmed populace; he denounced the danger involved in the use of the more deadly weapons; he condemned indiscriminate bombing, proclaimed the rights and supported the legitimate aspirations of the peoples; he extolled the true dignity of the workers; he defined, courageously and clearly, the principles and rules governing just peace; he called upon rulers and peoples to collaborate as brothers; he indicated the foundations for sound democracy; he proposed disarmament; he reminded strong and wealthy nations of their duty to help weak and impoverished peoples.

This rich collection of wonderful documents constitutes a *Corpus doctrinae* and a *Corpus iuris* which could be entitled: "Basic principles and rules for individual, family, social, national, and international peace."

Unfortunately, the Pope's voice often went unheard; his teachings were not always accepted; the path he traced out was not always followed. Nor was that all: some did not stop short at misrepresenting his words of truth, calumniating the absolute purity of his intentions, giving a sinister interpretation of his holy endeavours for charity and peace.

The Pope suffered bitterly, but he did not become discouraged nor give up his efforts.[11]

It was enough for him to know that he was carrying out his own duty as Father and universal Pastor. And so the volume of his discourses and messages, as though it were a monument erected to himself, will remain throughout the centuries as a witness to his lofty wisdom, both human and divine, to the undying glory of the incomparable Teacher and as a reproach to shame those who, deaf and unmoved, closed their ears and their hearts to his loving appeals.

Two great wars: two great Popes

It might be useful to compare the words and works of Benedict XV and Pius XII, the great Popes of the two world wars.

The substance is the same; both addressed to the world the same words of truth and justice; both worked intensely, with admirable charity, as peace-makers. There is nothing to be wondered at in this. The Church does not change, as the Gospel does not change.

Do you want an example? Who does not remember Benedict XV's famous words: " this useless slaughter "?[12] Pius XII, while recoiling from anything too crude in his expressions, is no less vigorous in a statement such as this: " No earthquake, no famine, no epidemic, no calamity caused by natural forces can be compared with the unimaginable load of sufferings which man brings upon his fellows when, rejecting love, he is swayed by hatred."[13]

But the frequency and the volume of Pius XII's words, and also of his external activity far exceeded anything that Benedict XV could say or do.

God sends His Church the men for the times. And the times were very different.

In the earlier period it was difficult for the Pope's words to reach the masses, also because what he said was often calumniously attributed to worldly designs. Where Pius XII was concerned, on the contrary, freed as he was from earthly rivalries, all peoples—with that happy intuition which is often the mark of popular feeling— seemed to look to him with confidence, to that one Chair, for the words of truth and life.[14]

Longing for peace

The central idea which at all times inspired the words and works of Pius XII, and the word most often upon his lips was: PEACE.

In 1939, only a few days before the war, he gave the warning: " Nothing is lost with peace. All may be lost with war."[15]

At Christmas 1957, Pius XII concluded with these words the last of his great messages " Peace is a good so precious, so productive, so desirable and so desired, that every effort in its defence, even with reciprocal sacrifice of legitimate individual ambitions, is well spend."[16]

The last word Pius XII pronounced in public was Peace.

On the morning of Sunday, October 5th, 1958, the Pope, in a state of utter exhaustion, addressed those taking part in the Congress of Latin Notaries. He concluded his address by exhorting his hearers to carry out the duties of their state as a contribution—he said—" to the preservation *of peace,* the desire of all men of good will."

He added: " The Church, which works with all her strength for the same end, cannot but rejoice."[17]

As Head of the Church, and on her behalf, Pius XII had indeed worked *with all his strength* for peace.

That day—tired out and almost at the point of death—he could have said of himself: " *to the utmost limit of strength and energy.*"[18]

It was his " *Consummatum est.*"

It was the close, in full consciousness, of a pontificate which, in a world constantly at war, had been a constant striving for peace.

" A river of peace upon the world! This is the desire which We have most constantly cherished in Our heart, for which We have most fervently prayed and worked, ever since the day when God in His goodness was pleased to entrust to Our humble Person the exalted and awe-inspiring office of Common Father of all peoples."[19]

These words are from the Christmas Message for 1954, which was published only on January 3rd, 1955. In December, the Pope was seriously ill.

During those days of acute suffering, he must often have gone back in thought over the fifteen years of his troubled and torturing pontificate.

It was then that he wrote the words we cannot read today without deep emotion: "Casting a glance backwards over the years of Our pontificate ... We feel that it was the intention of Divine Providence to assign to Us the particular mission of helping, by means of patient and almost exhausting toil, to lead mankind to the paths of peace."[20]

Today, a year after his passing, we can bear solemn witness before the world to the generous, unreserved and heroic fidelity with which Pius XII fulfilled his great mission.[21]

SOLITARY
AMONG THE MULTITUDES

How often, when my thoughts have returned to Pius XII, the words have come to my mind with which St. Paul described himself and his apostolate: " *Segregatus in Evangelium Dei.*" [22]

Segregatus: Pius XII was indeed " separated ": separated from all men and from all things. Not that he was aloof or indifferent, but he saw all men in God, and he judged and carried out all things with God and for God.

By nature he was almost irresistibly inclined to withdraw within himself, to cut himself off from others.

He had an intense love for study; he was happy when he was sitting at his desk, surrounded by books, reviews, and documents. [23]

His keen intellect gave him ready access to the most varied and difficult subjects: his impregnable memory furnished him, you might say, at every step with a wealth of information, of studies, of facts. This was the secret of his amazing facility in relating one event to another, one question to another, present circumstances to those of other days.

51

The result was a clear and comprehensive vision of reality; the consequence, wise and carefully weighed decisions.

He did not like to make up his mind immediately.

When asked to do so, he did not conceal his embarrassment; he became silent, thoughtful. He was not only slow in finding a solution on the spot, but, when it came to formulating the solution, he seemed to have difficulty even in choosing his words.

In the end he was still not satisfied and sometimes, by telephone,[24] he would give a completely different solution.

If, on the contrary, he was given time to study everything quietly, for instance, if in the evening he was sent a note (accompanied, of course, by all the necessary documentation),[25] the next morning, with complete serenity and the most apt expressions—obviously the fruit of prolonged reflection—the Pope would announce his decision with exactitude and clarity.

A tireless worker

He had a phenomenal capacity for work. He would spend hours and hours, almost without interruption, until late at night, calm and recollected, reading, meditating, making notes, and showing no sign of fatigue.

He read with extraordinary rapidity, and at the same time with such attention that he would immediately grasp the salient points of a document or a problem.

Time and again I wondered what was the secret of that amazing capacity.

The secret lay in method. He had accustomed himself to dealing with every question as though it were to be the only object of his study. He would give complete attention to what he had before his eyes, without worrying about all the other papers awaiting their turn. Their turn would come, inexorably; but in the meantime, the enormous volume of the work to be done did not rob him of his calm and serenity (as it often does with others) in the work that he was actually doing.

What was the source of such tranquillity? Self-control? The triumph of a will steeled by effort? The joy of quiet, hidden toil? The certainty of being able to withstand till the end these long and exacting labours?

Perhaps all of these qualities. But above all, his complete mastery of himself which found in turn its source and support in his total surrender to God, in his will to sacrifice his life for God's glory.

It has been said that study is prayer. Rarely has this axiom been so perfectly verified as in the case of Pius XII.

Only in this way can we explain the fear—or rather, the scrupulousness—about losing a single minute of his time, which made him deny himself needed rest and give up even those moments of relaxation which are of such help in renewing energies. Even the time given to the daily walk, required by the doctors,[26] was kept for reading.

Pius XII unwittingly described himself in a speech which he prepared but did not deliver, and which has remained as a kind of testament. It is a commemoration of Benedict XIV. Pius XII extolled, in words of admiration, the tireless activity of this great Pontiff, without realizing that he was writing at the same time, for posterity, a precious autobiographical document.

(Benedict XIV) " attended to the tasks of government "—wrote Pius XII—" with the utmost self-devotion and with a rare conscientiousness which made him treasure every scrap of time." The author of the " *Vitae et Res Gestae Romanorum Pontificum*, Romae 1751," a contemporary of Benedict XIV (Marius Guarnacci) already styled him *rigidus exactor temporis*, a definition whose vigour has been rendered by a present-day authoress: " his schedule was unmerciful."[27]

Pius XII, too, was "*rigidus exactor temporis*"; his schedule also was unmerciful.

One day he said to me: "You know what the doctors told me? That I lead an inhuman life." And he smiled as though he were satisfied.

The expression was too harsh. It was not that there was anything anti-human about that wonderful life; but we can indeed say that there was scarcely anything human left in it: all merely human cares, desires, and needs had been consumed and sublimated by the glowing fire of divine love.

Rather than inhuman, his life should have been called superhuman.

Happy hours

Pope Pius XII's natural leaning towards solitude found full satisfaction in prayer.[28] Those were the happiest, the most real and the most fruitful hours of his life.

The most beautiful and most expressive photographs of Pius XII are those which caught him in the act of prayer.[29]

The last was taken on Sunday, October 5th, 1958. It is perhaps the most precious of all.

The Pope is kneeling for the prayer to Our Lady of the Rosary. His face is pale, but his eyes are radiant, their gaze turned towards the altar. His figure is upright; his diaphanous hands are joined in petition. His whole being breathes serenity, gentleness, piety. A faint smile seems to play upon his lips, the smile of one already contemplating in foretaste the joys of heaven.

" My day "

The following Tuesday, October 7th, was the last day of the conscious life of Pius XII, for the attack on Wednesday morning deprived him forever of consciousness.

Three years earlier, he had said to one who was close to him: " I shall die suddenly. But I have asked Our Lord to give me a day to prepare." On the morning of that 7th of October, he said to the same person: " This is my day."

He asked to be given Holy Communion, which he received with the usual edifying devotion.

Then he became lost in God.

What passed between Jesus and His Vicar during

that last loving colloquy here on earth has been recorded by the Angels, but will never be recounted by man.

The prayer continued, intense, deeply recollected, as time drew on.

Never had Pius XII appeared and been, as he was at that moment, the great and holy " Solitary "!

The person attending him brought a little hot broth. The Pope, recalled to the reality of daily life, made a sign to wait.

More time passed, and there was no indication that the prayer would end. A second cup of broth took the place of the first, which was no longer hot. Another reminder, another gesture from the Pope: " Wait! " It was only after further insistence, affectionate but firm, that he finally drank a few sips. It was now the third cup, for in the second also the broth had grown cold.

Among the crowds

And yet this Man, who was inclined by nature, studiousness, devotion, and ascetism to solitude, was perhaps the Pope who had the greatest contact with the crowds and to whom they flocked most. Audiences, large and small, private and special, in the halls of the

Vatican, in St. Peter's, on the Square, in the rooms and the courtyard of Castelgandolfo: for twenty years they flowed on, ceaselessly, irrepressibly, endlessly.

People of all nations, all classes, all religions; politicians and children from Catholic Action; princes and plebeians; industrial magnates and workmen; scientists and illiterates—all gathered before His Holiness.

For them all, Pius XII, had words of kindness, encouragement, and exhortation.

But how much time those audiences took and what labour they entailed!

The Pope always prepared for them conscientiously. Everyone remembers the crowded general audiences at which the Pope himself read the list of the various groups present, greeting them all in their own tongue.

The enthusiastic applause expressed the appreciation of all concerned. But the mere reading of the list meant for the Pope—as he confided to me—an hour's preparation.

It is humanly impossible to calculate the immense good Pius XII accomplished by what I might call: *the apostolate of the audiences.* Long, numerous, and exhausting were the audiences; fervent, generous, and sanctifying the apostolate!

And the speeches?

They were the joy of the hearers, the cross of the orator. He was wont to recall what Pius XI had said to him: " Speaking almost every day, on so many subjects, is a heavy burden indeed."

Pius XI did not as a rule write his speeches or, at least, did not write them in full. He meditated at length and often made short notes. Then he left the rest to the inspiration and improvisation of the moment.

If he did not have the gift of flowing diction, he had the far more precious gift of deep thought, which was often original and touched with genius. In expressing his ideas, he liked to bring to the fore the newer, and so more interesting, aspects. As a result, his speech was slow, at times almost halting, with repetitions, broken and unfinished phrases. You could see that the Pope was composing his speech on the spot, seeking the right word, working on the sentences, clarifying clauses and references. In spite of the inevitable imperfection of the form, the ideas emerged clearly; the historical allusions were accurate and well-chosen.

The substance was solid, apt and beautiful, the fruit of wide culture, the expression of an apostolic soul.

Pius XII had his own method. He fully realized that he did not have the gift of improvisation.[30]

Every speech was for him a grave undertaking which seriously preocupied him.

His labours were threefold: preparation, composition, recitation.

The preparation involved, above all, study.

The subjects were most varied: religious, moral, social, pedagogical, juridical, scientific, philosophical, historical: sports, economics, industry, astronomy, astronautics, national and international politics, an almost unlimited range.

For his study, Pius XII chose assembled the most recent and authoritative publications. If necessary, he ordered them even from abroad.

All of this material—which was often very voluminous—would be carefully scanned and sifted by himself. I remember how, in the summer of 1958, going in for an audience, I noticed on a small table a weighty and imposing package of books. The Pope, who had not failed to note the object of my curiosity, said: " Look, all of those are books on gas."

And, in fact, on September 28th, 1958, he delivered an address to a congress for the gas industry.[31]

Twofold aim

Some may wonder: why all this labour?

It was maliciously insinuated by certain people that Pius XII wanted to appear competent and to give lectures, as it were, in every field, as though it were a matter of harmless, petty vanity.

Nothing could be farther from the truth. The Pope was too intelligent to entertain the illusion that, by studying for a few months, he could set himself up as a kind of rival to eminent scientists and specialists.

The truth is very different. Pius XII was wont to say that *the Pope must speak as Pope.*

In his approach to cultured men, his aim was twofold: on the one hand *apologetic;* on the other, *pastoral.* He wanted to show that the Church does not disdain the progress of the human sciences, since the Pope himself liked to keep up to date with the latest scientific findings. The findings of science, indeed, insofar as they are accurate and certain, not only are not in conflict with Catholic faith, but receive from faith light and confirmation.

61

The second, more important, aim was *pastoral*. The Pope first dazzled his admiring hearers with the harmony between science and Catholic teaching, and then, with skillful oratory, deduced the religious and moral obligations which arise for scholars in every field from a Christian understanding of their profession.

In this way, the references and explanations of a cultural and scientific character—often no more than a few simple allusions—served as a departure point for the flight towards the supernatural heights of the apostolic ministry.

World-wide repercussions

This pastoral aim was even more clearly evident when, especially on the occasion of official congresses, certain questions were submitted to him concerning the legitimacy and morality of particular teachings or scientific methods.

The questions raised were often of the greatest importance and were still a matter of controversy among scholars.

Pius XII studied, consulted, reflected, prayed.

His answers were clear and comprehensive. The general outline was, however, always the same: a scientific statement of the question, an explanation of Catholic teaching, an application of the teaching to the solution of the problem submitted, and lessons and exhortations for the religious and moral life of his listeners.

His hearers were left convinced, won over, deeply moved.

God alone knows the good that Pius XII did, at the cost of such labour, to many, many chosen souls whose activity reached out over a very wide radius.

In this way the Pope's teachings and the principles he laid down would often have world-wide repercussions.

Perfection
even in detail

The torment of preparation was followed by that of the actual writing of the speech.

Here again Pius XII's ideal came to the fore: to strive for perfection, even in detail.[32]

His extraordinary knowledge of languages enabled him to write fluently and correctly in various idioms.

At this point the dictionaries came into action: the most famous, the most complete and the most recent dictionaries.

He had a magnificent collection which he consulted most constantly to check, for instance, whether a particular word was the right word, whether or not it was archaic, whether there were more appropriate synonyms. In this way he had acquired a wide and sure knowledge of linguistic exactitude and purity.

More than once I had the experience of hearing the Pope say to me during an audience: "You see, my dear Monsignor, this expression is rejected by the purists." The audience, of course, was a private one. The purist ... was not me![33]

The quotations

Another point about which Pius XII took much trouble in drafting his speeches was that of the quotations.

Long experience as a scholar had shown the Pope how often quotations are inaccurate, even in the most excellent and highly reputed books. He would recall laughingly that Professor Scialoia once said to Professor Contardo Ferrini: "I congratulate you. In your last book—which is really excellent—I found one accurate quotation!"

A typical example is from 1948. Pius XII was preparing the speech he was to give for the thirtieth anniversary of the foundation of the Girls' Catholic Action

Movement. The idea occurred to him to quote a saying of Mazzini: "The Papacy is dead."

Pius XII was sure that he had heard and read this saying as a boy. But how was he to find the text in the pile of volumes containing Mazzini's complete works?

He consulted the experts, the most ardent and up-to-date specialists on Mazzini. The answer given him was that Mazzini had never said nor written those words.

The Pope was not satisfied. He continued his research and, finally, discovered Mazzini's words exactly as he had remembered them.

How happy he was that day!

The quotation was inserted in his speech of September 5th, 1948, with the greatest oratorical effect. When he asked those girls, full of life and high spirits, if they had come to Rome from all over Italy to pay homage to one who was dead—and dead for a hundred years!—the applause was deafening and the enthusiasm indescribable.[34]

Finishing touches

The speech, once written, was revised with the greatest care. The text was ready some time before the day fixed for the audience or broadcast. But, up till the last moment, Pius XII made corrections: changing words and phrases, remodelling periods, adding and removing clauses; the text only took its final form when the speech was actually given. At times, the Pope even made further changes on the proofs of *L'Osservatore Romano*, which he always corrected personally.[35]

Extenuating labour

Everyone remembers how Pius XII, during the first years of his pontificate, delivered his speeches from memory. He had a prodigious memory: what the psychologists call a *visual memory*. He used to say himself that, when he spoke, he saw the manuscript as though it were in front of him, and he turned the pages mentally.[36]

The Pope's memory never failed. But the use of microphones and loud-speakers and especially of radio made it advisable to read the text.

The reading also was carefully prepared, so that every sentence would be correctly enunciated. The result (apart from the natural gift of a clear and pleasing voice) was a good delivery, accurate and unhesitating pronunciation and a varied range of intonation, now soft, now strong.

66

This whole accumulation of efforts and labours helped to undermine the health of the great Pontiff.

From the start he had confided to his intimates that all these speeches represented a terrible burden of work. But, during the last months of his life, these confidences took on a plaintive note. There was practically no audience in which he did not complain of this to me.

In August 1958, he never stopped worrying about the number of speeches he would have to give in September: "Two or three every week," he would say "and sometimes one almost every day!" [37]

This was the voice of nature; all natural energies were now spent.

On this battle-field, the field of *his* apostolate, Pius XII fell gloriously.

Providential destiny

This man, whose mere presence stirred the crowds to joyful enthusiam, remained—as I have said—practically cut off from everyone.

Segregatus!

Such, it seemed, was his providential destiny. In his humility, he loved to mingle with others, but he could never simply be one among them, hidden among them. He was always on a plane above everyone else.

The more lowly he tried to be, the higher he seemed to rise. He bent down from his height towards each one; but no one rose up to his level. Few could be his equals in culture; very few in his heroic devotion to work; none—or almost none—in moral stature and virtue.

Even when he laid bare his soul with almost child-like simplicity, even when he smiled pleasantly and laughed happily in the course of delightful conversation, we felt that he was, indeed, *with us*, but never that he was *like us*.

His was a superiority that was self-evident, but not oppressive: it won hearts, but did not inspire fear. It was not an affected external attitude, but the irresistible splendour of inner radiance.

Pius XII made one think of a superhuman apparition: one of those exceptional human beings whom the Heavenly Father sends down to earth to turn men's thoughts towards the things of Heaven. His transparent body, his emaciated face, his gentle eyes, revealed, as through a light veil, the wondrous beauty of his soul. His dignified bearing, his gestures, his voice—deeply resonant and of youthful timbre—his whole being, in its aristocratic refinement, radiated a charm which inspired trust and veneration.

How often a word from him sufficed to restore peace to a soul, recall it to the path of duty, give new courage for the uphill road of life!

No one took leave of Pius XII without feeling deep joy at having met him and the highest esteem for his personality.[38]

The words of Holy Scripture come to mind here: " O Lord, great art thou, and glorious in thy power ... they that fear thee shall be great with thee in all things."[39]

MILD AND HEROIC

A mild disposition

Pius XII was, by temperament, mild and rather shy. He was not made to be a fighter.

In this he was different from his great Predecessor, Pius XI, who, at least as far as outward appearances go, relished a fight.[40] Pius XII, on the contrary, suffered, and showed it.

This inclination to prefer solitude and tranquillity naturally disposed him to avoid rather than to face the battles of life.

In his goodness he endeavoured to please everyone and displease no one; he preferred the ways of sweetness to those of severity, persuasion to command.

In the candour of his soul he did not even suspect that others might be wanting in truthfulness or sincerity. Humble as he was, he thought that everyone was like himself: as genuine,[41] as disinterested as he was.

At times, in more difficult moments, his keen intelligence and sense of detail brought to his mind, rapidly and clearly, all possible solutions. He immediately saw the *pro* and the *contra* of each one, the advantages and disadvantages, the possible consequences both favourable and unfavourable. And so he was perplexed, hesitating, as though he were not sure of himself.

He needed time for reflection and for prayer.

But he was not always given time.

One would suggest this, and another that. Each one claimed—as usual—to have found the right way, the only way, the way the Pope should have followed.[42]

All this left him troubled.

Once a decision had been taken, the next step was to carry it into effect: this was another delicate phase, especially if the decision was likely to be displeasing to anyone. If this were the case, Pius XII liked—as he said—to " sugar the pill." Taking the document which had been prepared, he would eliminate one or another clause that he found too strong, insert some more pleasing expressions, add a few words of praise.

The resulting pill was so skillfully sugar-coated that the patient, on reading the document or being received in audience by the Pope, would sometimes absorb *the sugar* with relish and not even notice he had swallowed the pill.[43]

At this point we may wonder: " Is it possible for a man, not only to conquer himself, but even to destroy, to obliterate completely natural dispositions received at birth?"

I think the answer is no.

Granted human frailty, something of one's natural temperament will always remain in the depths of the psyche, and there will be times when it will rise even to the surface.

Moreover, anyone who is in a high position, will not infrequently meet with one or another—out of the number of those who approach him—who will skilfully contrive to turn innocent natural weaknesses to his own advantage or to exploit them in favour of his ideas or his friends.

It was not possible even for Pius XII to be completely exempt from this common law of human existence.

In his exquisite courtesy, the Pope wanted everyone who was received in audience to take away a pleasant memory.

It happened quite often that he was asked to grant on the spot various requests for favours, permissions, dispensations: requests which were as insistent as they were indiscreet.

Pius XII would not have wanted to say yes, but there were times when he could not say no. After the favor had been been granted, these visitors did indeed go away satisfied.

But the Pope was not satisfied. His clear-sighted conscience was already possessed by the fear of having granted too much, or given in too quickly and made too great an exception.

He seemed anxious and troubled; he confided his anxiety to his intimates, as though asking their help to repair the damage in one way or another.

If something was able to be done about it, the Pope was visibly grateful, as though delivered from a nightmare.

Under these circumstances, the Holy Father Pius XII came rather to dread receiving high ecclesiastical dignitaries and priests.[44]

Do not misunderstand me: it was not that he was afraid of entering into discussion on all the different subjects he knew so well and was always ready to discuss. But he was afraid of himself, afraid that he would not be able to say no to the many requests of every kind, made insistently and persistently.

As a result, during his pontificate, direct and personal contact became less frequent between the Supreme Pastor and the pastors of the various dioceses: contact which would not only have been very useful in itself, but would certainly have afforded the prelates concerned a happy opportunity of benefiting by the Pope's wisdom, of rekindling their zeal at the flame of his apostolic ardour, and of pouring their troubles and doubts into the Father's heart, to draw therefrom comfort, courage, and new strength.

Nominations

Another torment for Pius XII was the making of nominations; the problem involved was more delicate—and the appointment more greatly desired!—the higher the post concerned.

On such occasions, of course, there is never any lack of claimants, not to say suitors, who, measuring, as it were, their personal worth by the extent of their ambitions, imagine they have certain capacities and lay claim to imaginary rights. On certain rare occasions, these not very edifying ambitions may even take convenient shelter and find benevolent protection between the silken folds of flame-coloured mantles.

In these difficult situations, between conflicting proposals and recommendations, Pius XII was ill at ease, torn between his natural affability and courtesy and the stern dictates of his conscience.

For this reason the Pope did not like making changes and preferred to postpone the decision.

A certain stagnation resulted in the Roman Curia, such as occurs in a body when irregularities begin to be noticed in the blood circulation. We older men continued to block the passage against the upward flow of fresher and more robust energies.

For this reason, it is not hard to understand the torture (the word is not too strong!) that Pius XII went through in preparing a consistory. It took months to draw up the list.

In May 1952, he spoke to me for the first time of the consistory which was later announced in November.

The labour of this long and painful gestation may partly explain why Pius XII preferred consistories in which many Cardinals were appointed, but which occurred very rarely: twice in the twenty years of his pontificate.

I should like to recall here also another characteristic trait of Pius XII: a trait deriving partly from his fear of placing others in an unpleasant situation and partly from his desire to satisfy their wishes.

During the twenty years of his pontificate, Pius XII never forced anyone to accept a nomination. At the very most, he would let the person concerned be told that his acceptance would give the Pope pleasure.[45]

Giant stature

I felt it my duty to mention these facts, but it must not be thought that I have wanted in any way to belittle the giant stature of Pius XII. I have simply tried to be sincere, for I am convinced that the great Pontiff would not have liked me to flatter him in death, after admiring, venerating, loving, but never flattering him when he was alive.

Man, however, is what he is. Grace builds upon nature; good will achieves, with God's help, great victories.

Yet there is a limit beyond which human possibilities cannot go. St. Paul himself said, after describing his interior struggles: "What I do is not what I wish to do, but something which I hate."[46]

Three ideals

In his hard, spiritual combat, Pius XII was guided and sustained by his ardent piety towards God, his tender devotion to the Blessed Virgin, and his exalted idea of the Papacy.

These were the three stars which lighted his arduous way, the three sources from which he drew strength and constancy, and which gave rise, as it were, to the three main points of the programme of his pontificate.

He formulated these points for me shortly after his election:

1. The new translation of the Psalter, to enable the clergy to understand and enjoy more fully the beauties of their daily liturgical prayer;

2. The definition of the dogma of the Assumption;

3. The excavations at St. Peter's Tomb.

Three decisions which were really daring.

The first modified a tradition that went back for many centuries.

The second involved long and serious study in the field of patristics, liturgy, and theology, and implied (according to the wish and the actual practice of Pius XII) consultation with the whole episcopate.

The third presented tremendous difficulties not only of an historical, topographical, and archaelogical character, but even from a technical point of view, since it called for extremely difficult and dangerous work under the main altar of St. Peter's Basilica, close to the massive columns supporting Michelangelo's dome.

The revised Psalter was published on March 24th, 1945.

The definition of the dogma was solemnly promulgated on November 1st, 1950.

The valuable findings of the Vatican excavations were announced by the Pope himself in the Christmas Message of December 23rd, 1950.

In short, three great aims and three great victories.

Our Lord granted Pius XII the grace to go far beyond his initial programme. He continued, however, to steer his course above all in the luminous wake of his three great ideals.

His fervent piety suggested the mitigation of the law for the Eucharistic fast in vigour for over a thousand years, the permission for evening Mass, the new Holy Week liturgy, the reform of the Breviary which is already under study. All of these were decisions as providential as they were revolutionary.

His genuine and trustful devotion to the Blessed Virgin inspired the consecration of the world to the Immaculate Heart of Mary, the solemn Coronation, in St. Peter's of the venerated image of Mary " *Salus populi romani* ", the institution of the feast of the Queenship of Mary.

His lofty idea of the Papacy—which was no exaltation of his own person, but meant the sacrifice of himself for the prestige of a God-given institution—gave rise to the canonization of Pius X, the beatification of Innocent XI, the resumption of the cause of Pius IX, the solemn commemoration of Gregory VII, the address in memory of Benedict XIV—which, as we have said, he left in written form—and, finally, the preparation of the Ecumenical Council, at which, in accordance with his instructions, a select group of learned ecclesiastics were working for several years.

" *Terrena non metuit* "

The virtue Pius XII admired most in saintly popes was fortitude: the virtue of which, in his humility, he felt the greatest need and which was the object of his constant striving.

He disclosed this himself on June 2nd, 1948, the feast of St. Eugenius, in his address to the Cardinals:

" *Terrena non metuit*. He feared nothing on this earth! This is the characteristic trait which sums up the life and work of all the great popes, the title to honour that the Church has chosen for all the popes who were saints. From the first moment in which, notwithstanding Our unworthiness, We were called to succeed them, We have felt that this trait should be a perpetual reminder for Our own conduct; We have made it the ideal which, with all Our weak strength, We must strive to attain. At a time like Ours, troublous and troubling, at a time when truth and error, faith in God and denial of God, the supremacy of the spirit and the sway of matter, human dignity and the abdication of man's dignity, ordered reason and irrational chaos are brought face to face in decisive struggle over the whole surface of the globe, the mission of the Church and of her visible Head can only be carried out and come to fulfilment under the motto: *terrena non metuit*. Be afraid? Of what? "[47]

And he added, as though asking for an opinion about himself: " Are We not strong? "

To this question we can answer. Yes. Pius XII was strong. He did not fear criticism, opposition, complaints, or accusations. We saw him go forward calmly and surely along the road that God and his conscience pointed out for him.

He did not even hesitate to take upon himself, entirely, the outward responsibility for the supreme government of the Church.[48]

" I do not want collaborators, but executives," Pius XII said to me, on November 5th, 1944, when he advised me that he did not intend appointing a successor

83

to the lamented Cardinal Maglione. It was an act of courage, even if one element entering into the decision may have been fear that his gentle disposition would let him be too easily influenced by others, or his kindly courtesy lead him to follow suggestions with which he might not always be fully in agreement.

In this also Pius XII was the great " Solitary."

Alone in toil, alone in battle.

The fighter

From the time he was raised to the supreme Pontificate, the Angelic Pastor had unceasingly to battle.

At Christmas, 1939, he said: " We have had to witness, to Our sorrow, a series of acts which are irreconcilable either with the prescriptions of positive international law or with the principles of the natural law and even the most elementary humanitarian sentiments:—premeditated aggression against a small, industrious, and peace-loving nation, on the pretext of a threat that is neither real nor intended nor even possible;—the atrocities (by whichever side they were committed) and the unlawful use of means of destruction even against non-combatants and those in flight, against old people, women, and children;—contempt for man's dignity and freedom and for human life; increasingly widespread and systematic anti-Christian and even atheistic propaganda, especially among the youth."[49]

The small nation, savagely attacked, was Finland.

It is well to note, however, that these words of bold censure were equally directed against Hitler who had invaded Czechoslovakia [50] in March, and in September, together with Russia, had attacked and devastated Poland.

A few months later, Hitler sent to Pius XII the arrogant von Ribbentrop. Was it to probe the Pontiff's dispositions? To intimidate him by vaunting the military power of the Nazis?

The Pope took the opportunity to protest solemnly against all the abuses of power for which Nazism was responsible in its relations with the Church.

The official was taken aback; he made some cutting remarks about the various religious denominations and ended by saying that he himself was impartial, since ... he had no religion and was therefore in a position to judge them all. The Pope's reply naturally met the case, and immediately afterwards he related to me the whole tragi-comic episode.[51]

Mussolini dared to send the Pontiff a strong message which sounded like a rebuke, and even a threat. Pius XII serenely replied that, to do his duty, he was ready to go to a concentration camp.

Rome was occupied by the Nazi troops.[52] The rumour went round that the leaders were preparing to transfer the Pope forcibly to Germany. Pius XII was not disturbed and did not even give up his daily walk in the gardens. The Vatican authorities, however, did get worried. Palatine Guards, Swiss Guards, Noble Guards occupied the ... strategic points, in readiness to defend the Pope. Pius XII thanked them and smiled. What could this handful of courageous and valorous men have done against the armed violence of the Nazis?

Teacher of truth

Pius XII's apostolic daring is evidenced, however, most frequently and most clearly in his discourses and messages. Even the great Pontiff's purely doctrinal teachings could often be called a form of combat. We need only recall the Encyclical *Humani generis*, which will remain as a document of the utmost importance on the level of the famous Encyclical *Pascendi*, in which St. Pius X condemned Modernism.

Considering only his discourses and messages, a rapid glance through the twenty volumes in which they are contained will leave the reader in admiration of the elegant prose and the carefully phrased, harmonious, Nineteenth century periods.

In Pius XII's style there is a rich profusion of phrases and clauses, as though he were trying to analyse even the most hidden recesses of his thought. At times, he is like a jeweller intent on showing to others the changing tints and manifold facets of a precious gem.

The precious gem is there, but it will be found only on a careful reading of the texts. In the profusion of this elegant phraseology, there are, indeed, a certain number of sentences which could not be clearer, more incisive, nor more powerful. In these we have the substance and the kernel of Pius XII's thought, while the rest are, to a great extent, a development, an amplification, and an ornamentation of these essential thoughts.

I shall give a few examples, by way of illustration, to incite and encourage others to do more careful research and make even happier discoveries.

In the following, Pius XII passes judgment on the situation and the evils of the present-day world.

" *There is a whole world to be remade from the very foundations; from savage to be made human, and from human, divine, that is, after God's heart.*"[53]

87

" *Human society is not a machine, and it must not be made such, not even in the economic field.*"[54]

" *At the root of present-day evils and of their deadly consequences ... (there is) the lethargy of the spirit, the anaemia of the will, the frigidity of hearts.*"[55]

" *All reality is from God: the divorce of reality from its principle and end is at the root of every evil.*"[56]

While the words: " Liberty and peace " are resounding amid general enthusiasm, the Pope sounds a warning note:

" *These words ... have been usurped as the monopoly of professional agitators and worshippers of sheer force.*"[57]

" *The only ideal liberty is that which refrains from all license, that liberty in which consciousness of one's own rights is linked with respect for the liberty, the dignity, and the rights of others, and which implies a sense of personal responsibility for the common good.*"[58]

" *True peace is not a kind of mathematical result of a balance of forces, but in its ultimate and deepest meaning, a moral and juridical process.*" [59]

" *The crux of the problem of peace is ... of a spiritual order, it lies in a spiritual shortcoming or deficiency.*"[60]

Speaking to the workers, Pius XII gave these reminders:

" *Work is a service rendered to God; it is a gift of God; it gives vigour and fullness to human life; it merits eternal rest.*"[61]

" *To the workers We say: the Church is with you, when you take action against unjust contracts or demand that just obligations should be fulfilled; She will be with you when you work by legitimate means for the betterment of your lot; but the Church could not be with you if what you asked should be unjust, or if you tried to obtain it by unlawful means; She could not be with you if you rallied to the enemies of God, sacrificing your souls, your liberty, peace, fatherland, and family; if, at the instigation of those who pretend to love you, you sowed hatred and practised violence.*"[62]

Pius XII's stinging rebukes were directed in a special way against the apathy of Christians:

" *In the world of today, a deeply Christian sense is all too rare; too few are the true and perfect Christ-*

ians.   It is men themselves who place obstacles in the way of the order willed by God."[63]

" *Beneath the surface of very real political and economic difficulties there lies a more serious spiritual and moral distress: the multitude of the narrow-minded and the mean-spirited, of the egoists and " opportunists," of those who run after the man in the public eye, who let themselves be swayed—be it illusion or faint-heartedness—by the sight of the masses, the clamour of public opinion, the heady wine of sensation.   Left to themselves they would not move a step to go forward resolutely—as would be the duty of living Christians—guided by the spirit of God, in the light of eternal principles, with unshakable trust in God's Providence. Such is the real, the inward distress of peoples.*"[64]

Vigorously Pius XII calls upon priests to practise the charity of Christ:

" *There may be priests who lack the gift of eloquence. It is possible to have an apostolate without eloquence. An apostolate without love is a contradiction in terms.*"[65]

In the political field, Pius XII's statements drove home their point with equal force and clarity.

90

EUROPE. " *Europe ... still awaits the stirring of her own conscience* "—that is, of her Christian conscience.[66]

EUROPE AND THE COLONIAL PEOPLES: " *... among some peoples until now considered colonial, the process of organic maturation towards political autonomy, which Europe should have guided with discernment and care, was rapidly turned into outbreaks of a nationalism greedy for power. It must be admitted that even these unforeseen conflagrations are, at least in part, the fruit of her own bad example.*" [67]

THE " FREE WORLD ": " *This is the weakness, all too widespread, of a world which likes to call itself pretentiously the free world. It is deluding itself or does not know itself: its strength does not lie in true freedom.*"[68]

THE COLD WAR: " *... the splitting of mankind into powerful and opposing blocs, whose life and action are governed by an ultimate law of radical and invincible mistrust: tragic paradox and course of our times.*"[69]

" *... the principal foundation on which the present state of relative calm rests is fear. Each of the groups into which the human family is divided tolerates the existence of the other, because it does not want to perish* *itself. While the fatal risk is averted in this way, the two groups do not live together; they co-exist. It is not a state of war, but neither is it peace; it is a cold calm. Each of the two groups is goaded by fear of the other's military and economic power; in both there is keen apprehension of the catastrophic effects of the latest weapons."*[70]

THE POST-WAR PERIOD: *" One fact remains beyond all doubt: up till the present, the fruits of the victory and its repercussions have not only been unspeakably bitter for the vanquished, but have proved a source of manifold anxieties and dangerous divisions even for victors."*[71]

CERTAIN " TALKS ": *" What is the use of discussion without a common language? How is it possible to meet if the paths are divergent, that is, if one party obstinately rejects or denies the universal absolute values, thereby making all ' coexistence in truth' unattainable? "*[72]

TRUE POLITICS: *" Experience should have taught everyone that politics are never more realistic and more concrete than when they are directed towards the eternal truths and the laws of God. Political realists who think otherwise produce only ruins."*[73]

92

THE CHRISTIAN STATESMAN: " ... *a Christian statesman may not—today less than ever—aggravate social tensions in his own country by dramatically emphasizing them, neglecting a positive approach to problems, and allowing himself to lose sight of a just estimate of what is reasonably possible.*"[74]

" ... *the Christian statesman does not serve the cause of national nor, in consequence, of international peace when he leaves the solid ground of objective experience and clear-cut principles and turns himself, as it were, into a divinely inspired herald of a new social order, creating even greater confusion in already wavering minds.*"[75]

I shall conclude this brief anthology by reading, for our common edification, two terrible invectives uttered by the great Pontiff.

The date of the first is September 1st, 1943, when the war was at its height: " ... *woe to them who, at this dread hour, do not rise to a clear consciousness of their responsibility for the fate of peoples, who stir up hatred and strife between the nations, who build their power upon injustice, who oppress and torture the defenceless and the innocent...; the wrath of God will come upon them for ever!* "[76]

The second is from November, 1956, after the tragedy

93

of Hungary. "*In the name of religion, of civilization, and of right human sentiment, let there be an end to illegal and brutal repression, to threats of war, to rival claims between powers—things which change earthly life into an abyss of anxiety and terror, deaden the spirit and nullify the fruits of labour and progress.*"[77]

One or another hostile critic has remarked that Pius XII's discourses and messages are indeed rich in lofty wisdom and warlike ardour, but that, after all, they are no more than verbal displays.

Pius XII himself furnishes the reply to this shallow criticism: "*Truth, like man, has only one face; and truth is Our weapon, as prayer is Our defense and Our strength, and as Our access to men's hearts is through the apostolic word—a living word, open, disinterested, and coming from a father's heart.*"[78]

A great statesman

Now let me ask a question. Was Pius XII a political Pope?

Many have said so, some with ill-concealed suspicion and criticism, others by way of outright accusation.

If by politics we mean the science and art of ensuring the common good in national and international public life, we must unhesitatingly affirm that Pius XII's pontificate was indeed a political pontificate, of great, whole-some, and holy politics.

A man who, like Pius XII, made every possible effort, first to avert war and then to limit its unspeakable horrors, who spent himself to restore peace, whose wise counsel pointed out for rulers and peoples the ways of civilization and progress, such a man is assuredly an eminent statesman who has well deserved the gratitude of the whole world.

Pius XI said on one occasion that, when politics touch the altar, the Church has the right and the duty to intervene.

Now I ask you: have or have not politics touched the altar?

In many nations, throughout vast territories, political regimes and systems do not only *touch,* but even *attack* the altar. The Church is persecuted; Bishops, priests, and the faithful are in prison; churches are closed or profan-ed; every freedom is done away with; new and diabolical techniques are used to break down completely the psy-chological resistance of the unhappy victims, living per-sons whose personality is already dead.

Could Pius XII witness all of this in silence?[79]

Has not a Pope the bounden duty to denounce dan-gers to faith, to encourage the weak and the wavering, to support the good, to stigmatize violence and persecution? Who can deny the Pope's right to lament the sufferings of his children, victimized by others' cruelty, and to extol those who, out of love for the Church, have fallen as martyrs of the faith?

This was Pius XII's duty: and this he did until the very end of his earthly existence. His last great Encyclical, of June 29th, 1958, is a cry of love and suffering: love for the Chinese people, suffering at the persecution of the Church and the threat of schism.

It is true that in many other countries, in the so-called " free world," the altar has not been attacked.

But who could affirm that it has not been *touched?* Social injustices, national selfishness—no less deplorable than individual selfishness—worship of the idols of technology, practical materialism, racial discrimination, the break up of the family, the spread of immorality—none of this is in harmony with the law of Christ. But, whoever touches the law of Christ, touches Christ, touches the Church, touches the Pope.

That was why Pius XII rose up with apostolic zeal against so many evils, throwing light upon their causes and suggesting effective remedies.

Nor was that all. Pius XII's words were turned even against political parties. Not from any slightest desire to meddle in petty rivalries, but because of the harmful ideologies professed by the parties: materialism, atheism, indifferentism, secularism.

And the press? How often certain papers gave a sinister interpretation of the Pope's words and actions, attributed diabolical intentions and tactics to the *Angelic Pastor,* covered him with insults and calumnies! On these occasions, the press did not merely touch the altar, but seemed to be trying to break even the tables of the Law, transgressing (as His Holiness John XXIII said) all the ten commandments of God.

Against this tide of injustice, error, and mud, Pius XII raised his voice: he spoke in defence of the Church, he spoke with the competence of a judge, with the authority of a teacher, with the affection of a father. "The Church," he said, "rises up serene and calm, but resolute and ready to repel every attack. As a good mother, tender and charitable, She does not seek the combat, oh no! But, precisely because She is a mother, She is more steadfast, indomitable, unyielding, with only the moral strength of her love, than with any material strength, when it comes to defending the dignity, the integrity, the life, the liberty, the honour, the eternal salvation of her children."[80]

I shall always remember that night of anguish between the 8th and 9th of October, 1958.

Pius XII was dying and I was at his side. The Pope
was stretched out on his bed, gasping for breath, motion-
less; his eyes were closed, and the death-rattle seemed,
at times, as though it would suffocate him.

The agony had begun!

We called him with loving words; we whispered
ejaculations in his ear; we prayed for him, but he could
no longer respond. If any glimmer of consciousness
remained during that last night, his blessed soul was
surely lost in God.

But outwardly he gave no sign.

As those painful moments drew on, my thoughts
went back four years, to December 1954, when Pius XII
was in danger of death.

His sufferings were unspeakable.

The hiccup! He was torn by one, continuous hiccup:
a convulsive shudder which racked unceasingly his throat,
his chest, his whole body. He could neither drink nor
eat nor sleep.

And yet, amidst all these torments, his mind was,

as ever, radiantly clear. His serenity was untroubled; his piety was edifying.

He kept on his bed, and very often in his hands, the book of the Exercises of St. Ignatius. His delight, and the delight of his visitors, was the beautiful prayer, *Anima Christi, sanctifica me!* which he recited again and again with deep devotion.

He did not want to neglect his duty nor to interrupt his work. Our audiences were as regular as ever. His instructions were to *tell him everything.* The doctors', to *tell him as little as possible.*[81]

We were in a strange situation. To obey the Pope was to injure his health; to obey the doctors was to disobey the Pope. And he was already thinking about his Christmas message.

When he told me, I have to admit that I did not believe it. To me it seemed impossible for the Pope, in the state he was in, to have the strength to prepare a document to which he was accustomed to attach such importance.

I was wrong. Only a few days later, as soon as he was up and the long convalescence had begun, Pius XII wrote, almost at a single stretch, the inspiring and profound message on " coexistence " which will remain one of the most famous documents of his pontificate.

During the days of suffering, the Pope had tasted more intimately than over the ineffable joy of his union with Our Lord.

There has been talk of a vision.

" Dominus est ... "

It was Thursday, December 2nd, 1954.

That day I had my usual audience.

Immediately afterwards, I wrote a few notes. I shall read them in full—as they were hastily set down—to show how the Holy Father, although so ill, remained serene, and ready even for a joke:

" I went to the Holy Father at 12.45. The Sister asked me to go and later told the Pope—after telling me she would do so—that I had wanted this myself. When I went in to His Holiness, I apologized for being late and informed him that I had received two Cardinals. The Pope said: ' Lucky, you! ' I replied: ' But this time Your Holiness is lucky, too.' And I handed him two substantial cheques for Peter's Pence given me by Their Eminences. The Pope said: ' You are right, I am lucky too." [82] *He was on the couch. He seemed much worse. Every five minutes he felt sick and brought up a coffee-coloured substance (detritus, not blood). His spirit remained serene. He said: ' I can tell you: the*

*others might think it was a sick man's hallucination.
Yesterday morning, I clearly heard a voice (a clear
voice!)' and, as he spoke, the Pope touched his right
ear,' and it said: "Now there will come a vision." But
nothing came. This morning, while I was assisting at
Holy Mass,*[83] for an instant I saw Our Lord. It was only
an instant, but I saw Him clearly."*

I went out at 1.30 p.m.

Two days later, on Saturday, December 4th, I returned for an audience. This is what I wrote:

*"12.40. The Pope was in bed. He was satisfied with
the consultation. He was full of praise for the doctors
and said they had been very optimistic, especially Professor Paolucci.*[84] *He stretched his arms out wide, as he
does when he gives the blessing, looked up to heaven
and said: 'Voca me!' Then he added: 'I thought
Our Lord was calling me to Himself. Instead!...' He
picked up again the little book of the Exercises of
St. Ignatius and said: 'This is my consolation!'*

*Lying on his bed, pale and weak, the Holy Father
really gives the impression of a soul belonging wholly and
only to God."*

Who among us does not still see that magnificent and characteristic gesture with which Pius XII brought the public audiences to a close?

His tall and slender figure erect, the Pope turned his gaze up towards heaven. It was a gesture of *entreaty*.

His arms were thrown wide open as though he wanted to draw the whole of mankind into a fatherly embrace. It was a gesture of *blessing*.

But those wide open arms, those transparent hands with their tapering fingers stretched out, that body which seemed almost to stiffen gave the Pope the appearance of one crucified. It was a gesture of *immolation*.

Pius XII could have applied to himself the words of the Apostle: " With Christ I hang upon the Cross."[85]

In pain and suffering, as a conscious and willing victim, he was consumed in the holocaust of his daily sacrifice.

If his crown was a crown of thorns, the Cross was his support, his refuge, his consolation.

So once again, in the Church's radiant firmament, the Cross became for a great and holy Pontiff a throne of majesty, a chair of truth, a standard of glory and triumph.

NOTES
AND DOCUMENTS

1) Reverend Eugenio Pacelli signed the oath *de secreto servando*—compulsory for all those entering the service of the Congregation—on February 14th, 1901. The facsimile is reproduced here.

Quod si in aliquo casu me dubitare contingat de praefati secreti obligatione, in favorem ejusmodi secreti interpretabor. Sic Deus me adjuvet, et haec sancta Ejus Evangelia, quae propriis manibus tango. Hac die *14 Febr. 1901*

Eugenius Pacelli

On October 3rd, 1903, Reverend Eugenio Pacelli was appointed "*Minutante*" of the Sacred Congregation for Extraordinary Ecclesiastical Affairs. The draft of the letter was prepared by the then Substitute in the Secretariate of State, Monsignor Giacomo Della Chiesa, the future Pope Benedict XV. Pacelli is called "Professor" because he was at the time acting professor of canon law in the legal faculty of St. Apollinaris (cf. inset of facsimile).

105

In July, 1902, Rev. Eugenio Pacelli had taken his diploma at the Apollonaris with the highest possible marks in *utroque iure*, as we find recorded in the booklet giving the awards for that year.

Cum RR. DD. Ioannes Pioli *e Sem. Rom.*, Carolus Nikiel *e Coll. Polon.*, Eugenius Pacelli, Doctoris Lauream sint assecuti cunctis suffragiis, eos V. E. singulari praemio donandos decrevit.

Three years earlier, Rev. Eugenio Pacelli had taken his degree in Theology, also with the highest possible marks.

We reproduce here the reference in the printed list of awards for the year in question.

Cum RR. DD. Franciscus Comandini, Henricus Giovagnoli, Lucas Piergiovanni *omnes e Semin. Pio*, Iosephus Bonaccorsi, Christianus Ianssen *uterque e Soc. Miss. SS. C. I.*, et Eugenius Pacelli Doctoris Lauream cunctis suffragiis sint assecuti, eos V. E. singulari praemio donandos decrevit.

2) Cardinal Pacelli assumed the office of Secretary of State on February 9th, 1930. He used to recall how Cardinal Gasparri had advised him to follow only the more important questions, leaving all the others to the various offices. " If you don't," he said, " you will lose your skin in the process." The method he recommended was, in fact, his own. But

Cardinal Pacelli steered a very different course. He wanted to be kept informed of everything, and for nine years he accomplished an enormous task. For his subordinates, he was a great teacher and a sure guide. He was very particular even about the style of the dispatches and the outward presentation of typed script. If he found the slightest error in the typing, he sent the dispatch back to be corrected and only signed it when the correction had been made. He did this with the greatest courtesy, without ever a word of reproof or the slightest sign of annoyance. But deeds were more eloquent than words. Every evening we sent him a huge leather bag containing a pile of letters (at times as many as a hundred) for his signature. The following morning the bag would return to the office without fail. Inside there were two compartments: in one the Cardinal placed the letters which had been signed; in the other, those which had not been signed. Our nickname for the latter was the *infirmary*. The fewer the ... *infirm,* the happier we naturally were.

Besides being Secretary of State, His Eminence Cardinal Pacelli was Archpriest of St. Peter's and Camerlengo of the Holy Roman Church. At the death of His Holiness Pius XI, he assumed the important functions which are reserved, *sede vacante,* for the Camerlengo. While the dead Pontiff's body was exposed in the Sistine Chapel (February 10th-11th, 1939), Cardinal Pacelli personally accompanied the more distinguished visitors. Among these was His Excellency Galeazzo Ciano, who was at the time Foreign Minister. The Minister knelt

down beside the Cardinal and, when the latter joined his hands in prayer, he imitated the gesture. At that moment a photograph was taken, which later irritated His Excellency Ciano. He immediately ordered even the plate to be destroyed. This was done. The reader will be interested to see here a reproduction of this extremely rare photograph.

3) Pius XI seemed sure that Cardinal Pacelli would be his successor. In preparation for the high destiny awaiting him, he sent him as Legate to Buenos Aires in 1934, and the following year to Lourdes. In 1936, he wanted him to accept the invitation to go to the United States. Cardinal Pacelli would tell how he had informed the Pope of the invitation received and told him that he did not intend to accept it. But Pius XI replied: " *Your Eminence must accept.*" In 1937, Cardinal Pacelli was again Legate at Lisieux; in 1938, in Budapest. During Cardinal Pacelli's trip to the United States, Pius XI began to speak to me frequently about his Secretary of State. " *He works well and quickly,* " he would say. Once Pius XI said to me: " *I make him travel, so that the world will know him and he will know the world.*" Then he added—in the tone of conviction and solemnity he used for important matters: " *He will be a fine Pope!*"

Pius XI gave another proof of his prevision as to his successor during the Consitory of December, 1937. On Wednesday 15th, at the ceremony of the imposition of the biretta on the new Cardinals, Pius XI referred to the fact he was now 81 years of age and said that this might be his last Consistory. Then, with reference to his successor, he added that perhaps: " *Medius vestrum stetit quem vos nescitis* " (in your midst there is standing one whom you know not). These words and the whole ample flow of the Pope's words gave us to understand—for me, and I was present, there was no doubt about the matter—that the Pope was pointing out his successor among those who were in the hall of the Consistory (that was why he said: *Medius vestrum*—in *your* midst). But, in the hall, there were not only the five new Cardinals (Piazza, Pizzardo, Hinsley, Gerlier, Pellegrinetti), but also Eugenio Cardinal Pacelli, who had accompanied the newly-elected as Secretary of State.—" *L'Osservatore Romano* " of December 17th carefully attenuated the episode and reported the Pope's sentence as: " *Medius vestrum est quem vos nescitis* " (amongst you there is one whom you know not), applying it to ... the whole of the Sacred College. The fact that, when a Pope dies, his successor is to be found among the members of the Sacred College and that you cannot know beforehand who it will be, is a matter of general knowledge. It would be hard to understand why Pius XI—whose speeches were so original and so personal—should have wanted to lay such stress on something everyone knew already. It would be equally hard to understand the *solemnity* with which the Pope expressed himself, going so far as to apply to himself Jesus' words to St. Peter: *Quid ad te?* What is it to thee?—If the Pope thought he had deserved Our Lord's gentle rebuke to St. Peter, it was simply because he was afraid of having gone a little too far in his previsions for a future which was not his concern.

By way of information, I reproduce here the extract from the Papal address as it was published in " *L'Osservatore Romano* " (Friday, December 17th, 1937):

" ... At this point the Holy Father remarked that his survey might be said to be complete; but he could not forget that, in addition to the places and the persons concerned, he had wanted also to recall a third aspect: the solemnity of the hour, which for him had a particularly solemn character, since during these days he had entered upon the second half of his 81st year. A great number of years and a matter of great importance, because time is a matter of great importance. Everything takes place in time: *omnia fiunt in tempore, in loco et in spatio.* Time, we may say without paradox, is eternity: time has been given to us to win eternity. This is so in a special way in the Pope's situation; for his this is a solemn moment, because at his age—no difficult calculation is necessary, and he himself is no prophet nor son of a prophet—, even though he says, as Leo XIII said before him, that he would not wish to set limits to the mercy and patience of God, it is certainly not far-fetched to think that the present Consistory may be his last. Even the number of the Cardinals would seem to indicate it, since there is only one vacant place. And another grave thought comes imperatively to mind, a thought which takes us back to the first Pope, the first Peter, the first predecessor of the present Sovereign Pontiff. John's words would now be applicable in the Sacred College: " *Medius vestrum est quem vos nescitis.*" But immediately there recur the Divine Master's affectionate words to Peter: " *Quid ad te?*: What is it to thee? Do thou follow Me: *tu me sequere.*"

111

4) Pius XII was deeply aware of the extraordinary importance of this period of the world's history and of the great mission entrusted by God to the Church and to its Head. In his Christmas allocution to the Sacred College, on December 24th, 1942, he said: " May we not perhaps compare the hour which is striking now for Christianity, for our faith which overcomes the world, to that of the first encounter between Christ and ancient paganism: an hour heavy indeed with grave dangers, but rich in magnificent promises and the hope of good things? " (*Discorsi e radiomessaggi di Sua Santità Pio XII*, Tip. Pol. Vat., Vol. IV, p. 322).

In his address to the Sacred College, on June 2nd, 1942, Pius XII had already spoken of " the raging tumult of this world, racked by the fever of a life and death crisis " (*Discorsi* etc., Vol. IV, p. 109).

In the Christmas Message for 1943, he said: " A time like the present—no less capable of mighty progress for the general good than of fatal errors and omissions—is perhaps without precedent in he history of mankind " (*Discorsi* etc., Vol. V, p. 164).

In his Easter Message for 1958, Pius XII attributed to " *something* (that) *has been barred from the clarity of God's life-giving light* " the cause of the grave evils that afflict mankind and which he admirably described:

" If private tragedies wound men's spirits, if scepticism and vanity wither so many hearts, if falsehood becomes a weapon in debate, if hatred flares up between classes and

112

peoples, if wars and rebellions succeed one another from end to end of the earth, if crimes are committed, the weak oppressed, the innocent placed in chains, if the laws are inadequate and the ways of peace obstructed—in a word, if this vale of ours is still furrowed by rivers of tears in spite of the marvels effected by the science and civilization of modern man, it is a sign that something has been barred from the clarity of God's life-giving light " (*Discorsi* etc., Vol. XX, p. 60).

In this unhappy state of affairs, Pius XII, in the address which preceded his Christmas Message for 1941, described the cares, the worries, and the struggles of the Church and of its visible Head:

" Venerable Brethren and beloved Sons, you who are Our closest and most trusted co-workers are capable of understanding and of measuring the tasks and duties, the cares and troubles, the sufferings and afflictions which, in these stormy times, weigh upon the shoulders and wring the heart of one who is called, in the inscrutable designs of God, to be a loving Father for all without exception, to give understanding and comfort in others' sorrow, to proclaim the truth without wavering, to watch vigilantly over that unity of spirit which God has willed despite all that may divide; one who is called, in the ceaseless tumult of earthly conflicts, tirelessly to affirm and to foster that brotherly feeling which is rooted in faith, in hope, and in charity. In the struggle for truth and justice, for goodness and holiness, for concord and peace, Our spirit does not and may not refuse toil and action, prayer and

113

sacrifice. We are the Vicar of the Prince of Peace, who brought peace and reconciliation to heaven and earth, making them one within Himself, and who from His cradle ushered in the reign of peace among men of good will. For the peace of the world, we have learned from Christ, from Peter and his Successors, to unite consolation and tribulation, to pass from Bethlehem to Gethsemane, to listen to the angelic choir hymning the glory of God and to the angel of suffering in his ministry of compassion " (*Discorsi* etc., Vol. III, pp. 313-314).

In his address of April 26th, 1958 to the Sodalities of Our Lady, the Pope again referred to the Church's mission in the present-day world:

" On various occasions We have pointed out, and We wish to repeat once again to you, beloved daughters, that men today are inclined to listen with renewed interest to the teaching which regards mankind as one body, and invites men to be but one heart and one soul.

" The mission of the Church today is to show that in Christ's teaching alone men can find salvation and new life for a world which is a prey to the nightmare of restless activity and unnatural din. Regard this then as your own mission, since you also belong to the Church and must live in the Church and work for her without respite and without delay " (*Discorsi* etc., Vol. XX, p. 119).

5) It would be interesting to make a careful study of the prayers written by Pius XII. It would reveal a characteristic

trait: in these prayers, in addition to expressing sentiments of genuine devotion, the Pope contrives to sum up, as it were, in a few words, certain points of doctrine and moral teaching. While revealing the piety of his soul, the prayers are thus also a proof of the solidity and depth of his thought.

We shall give a few examples.

The duties of a Christian wife and mother are wonderfully expressed in the " Christian woman's prayer to Mary, Most Holy Queen."

" Make us pure and blameless in thought and act; for our husbands, gentle, affectionate, and understanding helpmates; for our children, dutiful, attentive, and wise mothers; skillful in the management of our homes; exemplary as citizens of our beloved country; faithful daughters of the Church, ready to accept her guidance in thought and action " (*Discorsi* etc., Vol. XX, p. 542).

The " doctor's prayer " is a complete summary of medical ethics: " Grant that, following Thy example, we may be fatherly in our compassion, sincere in our advice, skillful in healing, averse to all deception, gentle in heralding the mystery of suffering and of death, above all, that we may be steadfast in defending Thy holy law of respect for life against the assaults of egoism and perverse instincts " *Discorsi* etc., Vol. XIX, p. 892).

All the duties of Christian politicians are summed up in the " prayer for Catholic members of Parliament."

" Great and eternal God, Creator and Lord of all things, supreme Lawgiver and supreme Ruler ... we ... implore Thy aid in a task that we want to accept and fulfil for the greatest spiritual and temporal welfare of our people.

" Grant us a sense of duty that will lead us never to omit any preparation or effort for the fulfilment of this high purpose. Grant us also that objectivity and healthy realism which will enable us to perceive clearly at every moment the course which seems the best. Grant that we may never stray from that sound impartiality which must make us strive for the welfare of all without unjust preferences. Grant that we may never fail in loyalty to our own people nor in fidelity to the principles we openly profess, and that we may ever have a spirit far above all possible forms of corruption or petty self-interest.

" May our deliberations be calm, marked by no other passion than that which is inspired by the holy yearning for truth; may our resolutions be in conformity with Thy commandments, even if the service of Thy will should mean for us suffering and renunciation. My we endeavour, even in our lowliness, to imitate the rectitude and holiness with which Thou Thyself dost govern and rule for Thy greater glory and for the true welfare of human society and of all Thy creatures." (*Discorsi* etc., Vol. XIX, p. 904).

6) *Discorsi* etc., Vol. VII, p. 357. It should be noticed that the Pope's prayer does not mention other aspects of suffering

(for example, its value as expiation and impetration), but is deliberately confined to stressing in what way and for what reasons suffering makes a soul holy.

7) Pius XII referred on several occasions to his own sufferings.

For instance, in the Christmas Message for 1949, in which, at the approach of the Holy Year, all were invited to the *great return* and the *great pardon*, the Pope described himself as a Father who *lives, toils, suffers, prays, and hopes.*

" Our invitation is meant, above all, as one of a father who lives, toils, suffers, prays, and hopes for the welfare and happiness of his children. And all men on earth are Our children, *saltem iure et destinatione*, even those who have abandoned Us, who have injured Us, who have caused and still cause Us suffering " (*Discorsi* etc., Vol. XI, p. 330).

8) In his speech, on Sunday, June 29th, 1952, to the sections for Rome and Lazio of the " *Opera dei Ritiri di Perseveranza* " (Organization for working-men's retreats and days of recollection), the Pope touched, in masterly fashion, on the joy of suffering:

" Remember the words of St. Peter which we quoted at the beginning: ' How ineffable your joy will be.' The fervent Christian should be joyful in the depths of his soul, joyful with an incomparable joy which suffering, toil, the uncertainty of the morrow cannot quench, for it comes from a supernatural security and rests in Jesus Christ. The good tidings of His coming amongst us, of His victory over the world of sin, of His real presence in the Blessed Eucharist: these are certainties which make it possible for peace, and even joy, to remain in the midst of the most serious difficulties " (*Discorsi* etc., Vol. XIV, p. 234).

9) Pius XII's serene joyfulness showed itself in private and pleasant conversation. Once, in one of his speeches, the Pope had quoted the text of the prophet Jeremias: " *Vox in Rama audita est.*" When he was correcting the proofs for " *L'Osservatore Romano,*" he noticed that, instead of *Rama, Roma* had been printed. Laughingly, he said: " *It must be an intelligent printer. He must have thought: What is this Rama? And, like a true Roman, he decided: What you need here is Roma!* " (Cf. *Discorsi* etc., Vol. II, p. 346).

Among his experiences during audiences, the Pope used to tell how, one day, he asked a little girl from Castelgandolfo how old she was. She answered: " I don't know! " When the Holy Father insisted, the little tot repeated: " I don't know! Daddy says one thing and Mummy says another." Then, when His Holiness asked her if she went to school, the tiny pupil earnestly replied: " Yes, I go to the kindergarten *for big girls!* "

Pius XII would sometimes recall laughingly other people's blunders in the use of foreign languages. For instance, one very high-ranking personality had referred, in French, to infectious and recurrent influenza (*la grippe*) as " une *brutte* maladie et *qui retourne!* " On another occasion, Pius XII had noticed that De Gasperi had said to the foreign press correspondents: " Nous espérons *supérer* les difficultés." The Pope remarked that the word which should have been used was " *surmonter.*" At times, Pius XII would tell some of his experiences from his long diplomatic career. For instance, when he was Nuncio in Germany, he was told of the case of an old Bishop who had completely lost his memory. Msgr. Pacelli took the opportunity of a celebration in the diocese to make a visit. He arrived on the eve of the feast. He was welcomed by the excellent Bishop with the greatest pleasure and affability. He had dinner with him and they conversed for a long time. Next morning, the Nuncio went to the solemn religious celebration. When it was over, up came the Bishop and said to him courteously and rather anxiously: " Good morning, Your Excellency! When did you arrive? Why didn't you come to see me? I want you to be my guest! " It was clear that the Prelate had forgotten everything!

Another episode. One day, Msgr. Pacelli, Apostolic Nuncio, was invited to dinner by a diplomat (Minister or Ambassador) of a small state. The worthy gentleman, in addition to his skill as a diplomat, had exceptional capacities as a ... cook, and this latter capacity would seem to have taken pride of place. During the dinner, the diplomat frequently rose from the table where his guests were sitting and walked away, whisper-

119

ing to the Nuncio, who was on his right: "*I am going to the kitchen to see if the dishes are properly cooked!*"

10) It may be interesting to recall the story of those telegrams. On the morning of May 10th, 1940, the Pope gave instructions to prepare a protest about Nazi aggression against neutral countries. His Eminence Cardinal Maglione *personally* wrote a short note for publication that evening in the "*Osservatore Romano.*" But the Pope did not think it was enough. In the meantime, the offices had prepared the draft of a letter from His Holiness to the Cardinal Secretary of State. This was ready at 8 p.m. But, to gain time, Pius XII had himself already composed the three telegrams, which were immediately dispatched.

I

Text prepared by His Eminence Cardinal Maglione

"Last night, Luxemburg, Belgium, and Holland were invaded, and over The Hague and Brussels, hundreds of aeroplanes are now sowing death from the sky among peace-loving populations which could and should have felt safe from the horrors of war thanks to the neutrality their Governments had proclaimed and jealously observed.

"We extend our deep sympathy to these sorely tried populations and commend the innocent victims to the infinite goodness of God. At the same time, we cannot but deplore the violations of international and natural law: by whichever side they are committed, they are a cause of horrors which fill the heart of every decent man with unspeakable grief ".

II.

Draft of a letter from H. H. Pius XII to Cardinal Maglione

Your Eminence,

From your intimate sharing in the anxieties and fears of Our apostolic ministry during these days of sadness, Your Eminence well knows how earnestly We have endeavoured, from the first outbreak of war, at least to ensure that the dread scourge should not fall upon other Nations.

Alas, our vigilant care proved vain, and We witnessed, to Our sorrow, the fear and distress of small Nations which, after trying in every way to preserve peace, one after another were beaten down against their will by the sweep of the avalanche, guilty only of being weak and of offering, in their neutral territory, possibilities of defence and attack for stronger belligerents.

And today, when we see three more small Nations, all hard-working, peaceful and peace-loving, stricken without provocation, attacked and invaded without reason, Our Father's Heart is bleeding at the thought of so many more thrown into mourning and of the terrible destruction brought

121

upon thousands and thousands of Our children. But, at the same time, We who guard and impart the Gospel teaching of justice, peace, and love cannot but raise Our voice to deplore once again the iniquity and injustice committed. We feel sure that Our sentiments find an echo in the hearts of all honest men. Confident that the violence which transgresses and tramples upon right, cannot destroy it, they derive from their faith in God the assurance that the supreme principles of truth, charity, and justice can alone provide a stable foundation for a civilization worthy of the name.

" With Our first Encyclical, We have already tried to recall not only Our own sons but all men of good will to these supreme principles. The more fragile and fleeting our earthly hopes may seem, the more earnestly, therefore, We invite each and every one to pray fervently and without ceasing to Him who is the God of peace, the Lord of those in power, the Supreme Ruler of peoples. May the Divine Mercy extinguish in men's souls the destructive flame of hatred and enkindle the regenerating fire of charity: may the evil designs of destruction and death be dissipated, and all peoples go forward towards the peaceful conquests of civilization and progress: overcoming incredulity and indifference, mindful once again of evangelical truth, may mankind return, contrite and trusting, to the Divine Redeemer in Whose name alone salvation is to be found."

III

Text of the three papal telegrams

Pius XII personally wrote the three texts on his small typewriter in the late evening of May 10th, 1940. He then corrected them by hand. A study of the changes he made in the telegram to the Grand Duchess of Luxemburg shows once again how carefully he always tried to make his writings more clear and more appropriate.

The plate opposite this page is a reproduction of the sheet of paper which the Pope signed and communicated for dispatch to the Offices of the Secretariate of State at about 8 p.m. that evening.

It is interesting also to recall another incident of those days. On May 6th, 1940, Pius XII granted an audience to the Crown Prince Umberto and the Princess Marie José. The Pope told them he was very worried about the situation of Belgium, fearing an invasion from one moment to the next. Princess Marie José was deeply disturbed and sent a special message to her brother, the King of Belgium. At 6.30 p.m. on May 8th, the Columbia Broadcasting System in New York gave news of a letter the Princess Marie José had written after her visit to the Vatican.

From the beginning of the hostilities, Pius XII was convinced that the war would be a long one. In August, 1940, he received in audience the Italian Ambassador, His Exc. Attolico, who said that, by now, the war was " won." The Holy

Father looked at him with one of those searching glances in which he could so clearly express surprise, disagreement, questioning, and merely replied: " Yes, it's won? " From the tone in which the words were uttered, the diplomat—a very intelligent man—realized that his optimism had carried him away and he corrected himself: " ... *practically* won." Pius XII often recalled the episode and smiled at the " *practically.*"

11) On more than one occasion Pius XII publicly complained of the misrepresentation of his words and the calumnies about his motives and his action in the cause of peace.

In the Christmas Message of December 23rd, 1950, he said:

" Nevertheless—as the height of injustice!—there are some, and they are well known, who accuse Us of wanting war, and of collaborating to this end with " imperialist " powers, which—they say—place their hopes in the might of deadly weapons of war rather than in the practice of right.

" What else can We answer to this bitter calumny except: Scan the twelve troubled years of Our pontificate; weigh every word uttered by Our lips, every sentence flowing from Our pen: all you will find are appeals for peace.

" Call to mind especially the fateful month of August, 1939. As the harassing dread of a disastrous world war grew ever stronger, from the shores of Lake Albano We raised Our voice imploring rulers and peoples, in God's name, to settle their disputes by mutual and sincere agreements. Nothing is lost with peace—We exclaimed—, all may be lost with war!

" Try to consider all this calmly and honestly and you will have to admit that, if in this world, torn by conflicting interests, there is still any secure haven where the dove of peace can tranquilly come to rest, it is here, on this ground consecrated by the blood of the Apostle and of the martyrs, where the Vicar of Christ knows no duty more sacred, nor mission more gratifying than that of being the unwearied advocate of peace.

" Thus We have acted in the past. Thus We shall act in the future, for as long as it shall please the Divine Redeemer of the Church to leave on Our frail shoulders the dignity and the burden of supreme Pastor " (*Discorsi* etc. Vol. XII, pp. 387-88).

Already during the world war, in the speech he gave on June 13th, 1943, to an " impressive and representative group of Italian workers ", the Pope had said:

" ... We are not unaware—and you yourselves can know from experience—that in these days when the life of the family and of society is burdensome and difficult, human passions take the opportunity to raise their heads and to provoke suspicion and the misrepresentation of words and deeds. So it is that an anti-religious propaganda is spreading among the people, especially the working class, the idea that the Pope wanted the war, that the Pope is providing money to keep the war going, that the Pope does nothing for peace. A more monstrous and absurd calumny has perhaps never been uttered! Who does not know, who does not see, who

has not means to ascertain that no one has worked more un-
remittingly than We have, in all the ways at Our disposal,
first to prevent the war from breaking out, and then to
prevent it from continuing and from spreading; that no one
has more constantly invoked and preached: peace, peace
peace!; that no one has endeavoured more earnestly to mitigate
the horrors of war? The sums of money that the charity of
the faithful place at Our disposal, are not destined and do
not go towards maintaining war, but are used to dry the
tears of widows and orphans, to console families tortured with
anxiety for their dear ones who are far away or missing, to
help the suffering, the poor, and the needy. The witnesses to
all of this are Our heart and Our lips. They do not contradict
one another, for Our deeds do not belie Our words. We are
aware also of the insidious lies which the enemies of God
spread abroad to trouble the workers and the people, seeking
in the sufferings of their daily life arguments against faith
and against religion, which is, on the contrary, the only consolation and the only hope that can sustain man on this earth
in his suffering and his misfortune. No. Our discourses and
our messages cannot be effaced by anyone nor distorted as to
their motive and their substance. All have been able to hear
in them words of truth and peace, and to sense the ardour
with which Our spirit is moved to bring tranquillity to the
world and enlightenment to those in power. They bear irrefut-
able witness that Our heart is bursting with an immense longing that the whole human race should know the ordered reign

of harmony upon this earth which has been given to man as a a place of sojourn on his way to a better and everlasting life.

" ... The evident reality of the actual facts and of Our own action will be sufficient to confound those who, with deceiving words, endeavour to throw upon the Papacy the responsibility for all the blood shed in the fighting on land and the destruction of cities, during the battles in the air and in the depths of the sea " (*Discorsi* etc., Vol. V, pp. 89-90-91).

In the Christmas Message of December 24th, 1947, he said:

" The position We take up between the two opposing camps is free from prejudice of any kind and from any preference for one or another people, one or another group of nations, as it is removed from any temporal motive. To be for Christ or against Christ: that is the whole question.

" You will readily understand, therefore, how painful it is for Us to see hostile propaganda misrepresenting Our thoughts and words, creating bitterness, hindering the peaceful exchange of ideas, widening the gulf between Us and so many souls redeemed by the blood and the love of the one Divine Saviour " (*Discorsi* etc., Vol. IX, p. 394).

In the address of December 27th, 1935, to the faithful of *Tor di Quinto* (Rome), Pius XII deplored the bewilderment caused among the people by the calumnies against the Church and the Pope.

(The indifferent and the enemies of Our Lord) " have forsaken God; they have become estranged from Jesus, from the Church, from the Priest. Some of these are today indiffer-

127

ent; others—it would seem incredible—have become enemies of Our Lord and are living in the chains of hatred; plunged in deep sadness, they do not so much as imagine that, by returning to the Father's house, they would recover the peace and the serenity they have lost. You are certainly acquainted with some such people; they know not what they do, and there is one main cause of their almost incomprehensible hatred and inexplicable aversion: the poison of calumny treacherously poured into their minds by unscrupulous men who systematically attack the Church, misrepresent the Pope's speeches, and give a malicious interpretation of his every gesture " (*Discorsi* etc., Vol. XV, p. 536).

The texts I have quoted clearly show how much Pius XII suffered from the calumnious interpretations of his words and actions. But this did not make the Pope stop or give way, as he pointed out with vigour and courage in his broadcast of December 24th, 1946:

" We are well aware that Our words and intentions run the risk of being misinterpreted or misrepresented for the ends of political propaganda.

" But the possibility of false or malicious comment of this kind would not suffice to silence Us. We should deem Ourself unworthy of Our Office, of the cross Our Lord has placed upon Our frail shoulders. We should feel We were betraying the souls which look to Us for the light of truth and for sure guidance if, to avoid evil interpretations, We were to hesitate, at so critical a time, to do all that is in Our power to rouse men's consciences from slumber and recall them to the duties of Christ's holy service.

"No right of veto, from whatsoever quarter, could prevail against Christ's command: 'Go and teach.' In unfailing obedience to the Divine Founder of the Church, We strive and shall continue to strive, to the utmost limits of Our strength, to fulfil Our mission as defender of truth, guardian of right, champion of the eternal principles of humanity and love. In the exercise of this duty of Ours, We may well encounter resistance and misunderstandings. But We are consoled by the thought of the lot which fell to the Redeemer Himself and to those who followed in His footsteps; and the humble, but trustful words of the Apostle Paul come to Our mind: 'I make little account ... of any human audit-day; ... it is the Lord's scrutiny I must undergo' (I *Cor.* 4, 3-4)" (*Discorsi* etc., Vol. VIII, pp. 352-53).

12) Benedict XV's appeal to the "Leaders of the Belligerent Peoples" reads thus: "this terrible struggle which every day seems more and more to be a *useless slaughter*."

13) *Discorsi* etc., Vol. XII, p. 8. To show the substantial identity between the teaching and action of Benedict XV and of Pius XII during the two world wars, we need only quote a few passages from a document which is little remembered today: the letter Benedict XV addressed to His Eminence the Cardinal Dean of the Sacred College on May 25th, 1915 (i.e.

the day after Italy had entered the war). In certain expressions we seem to hear the very accents so often recurring in the messages and discourses of Pius XII.

"Your Eminence,

... In Our first encyclical, moved by the supreme desire to see an end to the horrible carnage which dishonours Europe, We called upon the Rulers of the belligerent nations to consider how many tears and how much blood had already been shed and to restore without delay to their peoples the life-giving blessings of peace. 'Let those give heed,' we said, ' who hold in their hands the destinies of peoples. If rights have been violated, there are certainly other ways and other means of obtaining satisfaction; laying aside the weapons of war, let them have recourse to these, in sincerity of conscience and good will. Charity towards them and towards all nations leads Us to speak in this way, not any interest of Our own. May they not let Our voice, the voice of the father and the friend, fall upon the empty air.' But, We say it with a heart broken with sorrow, the voice of the friend and the father was not listened to; the war continues its bloodshed in Europe, and men do not even recoil from means of attack, on land and on sea, contrary to the principles of humanity and of international law.

"And, as if that were not enough, the terrible conflagration has extended also to Our beloved Italy, giving grounds, alas, to fear for her also that train of tears and disasters which is wont to follow every war, even when successful.

130

" While Our heart bleeds at the sight of so many misfortunes, We have not desisted from Our efforts to alleviate and diminish, as far as lay in Our power, the tragic consequences of the war. We give praise to God who has deigned to crown with success Our endeavours to obtain from the belligerent nations the exchange of the prisoners of war unfit for further military service. In addition, We have recently exerted Ourself, and with hope of success, on behalf of wounded or invalided prisoners of war not wholly unfit for military service, in order to render their lot less painful and to facilitate their treatment.

" But Our fatherly care has been directed, above all, to the needs of the soul, which are far more important than those of the body.

" ... The hour through which we are passing is one of sorrow; the moment is full of dread: but *sursum corda*. Let us raise our prayers more often and more fervently to Him in whose hands lie the destinies of the nations. Let us all turn with confidence to the sorrowful and immaculate Heart of Mary, most sweet Mother of Jesus and our Mother, that through her powerful intercession with her Divine Son the scourge of war may soon come to an end and peace and tranquillity return. "

14) Pius XII often spoke of the peoples' expectation of his words and of his conviction that he—and he alone—was the faithful interpreter of their feelings and aspirations.

In the broadcast appeal for peace of August 24th, 1939,

he said: "We entreat them (the rulers) by the blood of Christ, Who overcame the world by the strength of His meekness in life and in death. And, while We entreat them, We know and We feel that We have with us all those who are upright of heart, all those who hunger and thirst after Justice—all those who, through life's ills, are enduring already every form of suffering. With Us are the mothers' hearts, beating with Our own; the fathers, who would have to leave their families; the lowly, who toil and know not; the innocent, over whose heads the terrible threat is hanging; the youth, generous knights at the service of the purest and noblest ideals. And with Us We have the soul of this old Europe, which was fashioned by the faith and the spirit of Christianity. With Us is the whole of mankind, looking for justice, bread, freedom, not for the sword which kills and destroys. With Us is Christ, He Who has made of brotherly love His own, fundamental, solemn commandment, the substance of His religion, the promise of salvation for individuals and for nations" (*Discorsi* etc., Vol. I, pp. 306-7).

In the address to the National Association of the Grenadiers of Sardinia, on Sunday, November 6th, 1955, he said: "Among the signs which give for Our confidence" (in peaceful reconstruction) "We must mention the ever increasing flow of large and varied groups of people who are not satisfied with seeing and with being given just any word of encouragement and exhortation, but who ask to hear what the Pope has to say—what the Vicar of Jesus Christ has to say—on the

132

most different subjects. There is in this a holy desire to seek in Christ's teaching the principles for the solution of the problems which trouble individuals and peoples " (*Discorsi* ecc. Vol. XVII, p. 375).

Responding, on June 1st, 1946, to the congratulations of the Sacred College on the occasion of his name-day, Pius XII, in answer to the "*countless petitions*" forwarded to him, spoke in defence of the prisoners in the following terms: " We have already spoken about them recently in Our last Christmas Message and in the address delivered last February to the Diplomatic Corps gathered in Our presence. We readily acknowledge, of course, that during the months just past, large contingents of prisoners of war have been repatriated. If We return today to the subject of the hundreds of thousands of men who are still detained in prison and of the unfortunates who have no country nor even a roof over their heads, it is because We are impelled to do so by the countless petitions imploring Our intervention, and because this state of affairs calls imperiously for urgent and effective aid. On behalf of the prisoners of war, these manifold and earnest entreaties come from every class of society. They come from mothers yearning for the son who is far away; from wives who have come to the end of their frail strength and can no longer bear the burden of providing for the needs of a family; from children who look in vain for the heartening smile and the able hand of a father who will train and educate them to meet the harsh demands of life. Civil communities

133

and public authorities ask to have back the youth, the best energies with which to undertake and pursue that work of reconstruction in each particular country, upon which depends the general restoration of the international community " (*Discorsi* etc., Vol. III, pp. 106-107).

In the Christmas Message of December 24th, 1952, Pius XII said:

" The sorrowful chorus of prayers and pleas for help, far from decreasing as the lapse of many years since the world conflict gave good reason to hope, continues and becomes at times more intense on account of many and pressing wants; it rises towards Us, it may be said, from every part of the world and rends Our soul with all the distress and tears that it reveals " (*Discorsi* etc., Vol. XIV, p. 422).

In his last Christmas Message, of December 22nd, 1957, Pius XII, after his appeal for peace, added—as though by way of conclusion—: " We are sure that the peoples of the world are wholeheartedly in agreement with Us, and that they expect a like sentiment from their rulers " (*Discorsi* etc., Vol. XIX, p. 306).

15) Broadcast appeal for peace when the danger of war was imminent—August 24th, 1939 (*Discorsi* etc., Vol. I, p. 306).

16) *Discorsi* etc. Vol. XIX, p. 685.

17) *Discorsi* etc., Vol. XX, p. 435.

134

18) During that last speech, Pius XII was seen by all to be very weak and pale. He was holding his watch, which at a certain moment, fell to the ground. At the end, he took leave of his hearers with a significant: " *Adieu!* " Afterwards, he received in audience His Excellency Msgr. Dell'Acqua, who inquired anxiously how he felt. The Pope replied serenely: " *It is the end!* "

19) *Discorsi* etc., Vol. XVI, p. 331.

20) *Discorsi* etc., Vol. XVI, p. 331.

21) Pius XII was conscious of having done and of doing all that was in his power for the cause of peace.

" In imitation of the Divine Redeemer, ever since the Lord willed to raise Us in Our unworthiness, to the office of Sovereign Pontiff, We have left nothing undone to safeguard peace, to warn rulers and peoples of the dangers of war, to suggest procedures capable of averting fresh conflict, to limit and mitigate the disastrous effects of war. In all sincerity, We can indeed ask ourself: " *Qui est quod ultra debuimus facere, et non fecimus?* " (cf. *Is.* 5, 4). What is there that We ought to have done more, and have not done? " (*Discorsi* etc., Vol. XIV, p. 141).

In his address of September 7th, 1947, to the Men of Catholic Action, after affirming that he had always served the cause of peace, Pius XII explained what is meant by " serving peace."

" To the intercession of the Mother of God and of the Saints, We finally entrust that blessing for which all of you, the whole people of Italy and the great family of the nations are anxiously yearning: *peace:* no mere outward and juridical peace, but a real and just peace. As for Ourself—however the enemies of the Papacy, who yet remain the objects of Our love and good wishes, may distort Our motives and Our words—We have always served, and We shall always serve, as long as a breath of life remains in Us, the cause of true peace. Make of yourselves also, Men of Catholic Action, champions of this holy cause. To serve peace is to serve justice. To serve peace is to serve the interests of the people, especially of the lowly and the unfortunate. To serve peace is to look securely and steadfastly towards the future. To serve peace is to hasten the day when all peoples, without exception, laying aside rivalry and strife, will be gathered into a brotherly embrace. To serve peace is to serve civilized society. To serve peace is to preserve the human family from fresh and unspeakable misfortunes. To serve peace is to raise men's spirits towards heaven and to snatch them from the sway of Satan. To serve peace is to carry into effect the supreme law of God, which is a law of goodness and of love " (*Discorsi* etc., Vol. IX, p. 220).

On March 4th, 1956, responding to an address from the French Ambassador, His Excellency Count Wladimir d'Ormesson, he said:

" You were pleased, Mr. Ambassador, to recall Our efforts

May 9th, 1947

December 1st, 1956

January 21st, 1957

Last photograph of H. H. Pius XII (October 5th, 1958).

on behalf of peace. This is, indeed, one of Our most constant preoccupations. Since the day following Our election to the heavy responsibility of Supreme Pontiff, when We broadcasted a message to the whole world, until the present time, We have not ceased to raise Our prayers to heaven and to use the means at Our disposal in appealing to men of all opinions and all countries to seek unfeigningly this spiritual good, for which individuals and peoples are longing.

" Peace! Who can tell its worth and its blessings! May We have made it more keenly desired throughout the world, so that, to safeguard, preserve, and consolidate it, individuals and groups will henceforth be ready for more radical and more personal sacrifices. How We should wish men and nations to prefer it to the satisfactions of self-love and self-interest! How We wish that the pressure of public opinion would break through stubborn and unreasonable resistance, insist everywhere on the necessity for solving the most outspoken conflicts by friendly agreement and enforce acceptance of the arbitration and compromise through which so many irreparable evils could be avoided! " (*Discorsi* etc., Vol. XVIII, p. 5).

On November 6th, 1957, the Pope received the representatives of the *Lampada della Fraternità* and addressed them in these words:

" The World Organization of the Lamp of Fraternity ... affords Us, Gentlemen, in your persons a living image of what the world is longing for after the great international conflicts which have stained it with blood.

" Your group includes, indeed, together with your illustrious President, five Vice-Presidents each representing a continent. What more expressive symbol could there be of the desire for peace which, as We are prepared to believe, is gaining in depth despite the latent or overt hotbeds of war which are still all too numerous upon this earth.

" In the chorus of voices raised to insist at last upon brotherly concord between nations, the voices of those who have had to fight on behalf of each one of these nations have a special claim to be heard and to be heeded. Their valiant comrades who have died for the honour of the fatherland speak, as it were, through their lips; they themselves have experienced more keenly the horrors of war; and so now they seek to remain on the front of a peaceful combat and to win the victory over hatred, which divides peoples, over mistrust, which prevents agreements from being reached, over the greed and selfishness that subordinate a deep and lasting common good to narrow personal or national interests " (*Discorsi* etc., Vol. XIX, p. 561).

In his last Easter Message of 1958, Pius XII once again invited all Christians to heed his appeal for the cause of peace: " ... What good works more useful to the world can be done at the present day by all who are Christians than striving with all their energies for the firm re-establishment of just peace? Individuals and peoples, nations and states, institutions and groups are invited by the King of Peace to press on with confidence in this difficult and urgent task for the glory of

138

God. To this must be dedicated the whole rich store of intelligence, of prudence and, where necessary, of unflinching constancy, at the disposal of the Christian world, aided by all others who are genuine in their love for peace. Sincerity in wanting peace, readiness to make all the reasonable sacrifices it demands and honesty in discussing the problems involved, should naturally dispel the shadows of distrust. But if—which God forbid—that should not happen, it would finally be known to whom responsibility should be attributed for present discords. Be, therefore, a light of peace in this darkened world, and in every issue, God will be on your side! " (*Discorsi* etc., Vol. XX, p. 62).

22) *Ep. ad Rom.* 1, 1.

23) It was generally observed that Pius XII left very late for Castelgandolfo (as a rule, in the second half of July) and returned late to Rome (in the latter part of November). The reason for both delays was ... the books. Before leaving the Vatican, Pius XII carefully chose the books he would take with him. And it was no small number. Hard-working as he was and painstaking in his verifications, he always needed many volumes. In summer, when I asked him: " *Your Holiness, why don't you leave the stifling heat of Rome and get a little fresh air at Castelgandolfo?* " he would reply: " *What can I do, my dear Monsignor, I have to take so many books with me and I haven't chosen them all yet.* "

Once he was settled at Castelgandolfo and the books were

all arranged, it was not easy for him to make up his mind to go back, because it took a long time to collect all those volumes again. He had very little time to give to the operation, having an immense amount of work to do every day.

24) Pius XII made frequent use of the telephone. But he never said who he was. This gave rise to curious incidents. Once, for instance, he telephoned to the apartment of a Cardinal. The latter's valet, hearing an authoritative voice say: *" Call His Eminence for me,"* firmly replied: *" First tell me who you are! "* And, since the strange interlocutor would not tell him, the worthy fellow ... cut the connection.

One day, when I was at lunch with His Exc. Mimbela, then Ambassador of Peru, a servant came and told me with some annoyance: *" There is a gentleman on the telephone who wants to speak to you and will not say who he is."* Naturally—amid general astonishment—I got up and went to the telephone. It was the Pope. In this respect, Pius XII was very different from his predecessor, Pius XI, who used to display with satisfaction the elegant telephone installed in his study, and then add: *" Isn't it beautiful? But I never use it! "*

25) The documentation was always indispensable. Not infrequently the Pope would say to me afterwards: *" That summary is excellent. I read all the documents and I saw that nothing has been left out."* Sometimes the judgment was unfavourable: *" You see, the note did not take into consideration*

the contents of this document! " And the Pope would point to the ... evidence of the crime: the paper and the item which had escaped the notice of the zealous secretary. Only one who knows how voluminous the so-called " *posizioni* " (" *state of the case* ") can be (including reports, studies, telegrams, reviews, newspapers, etc.) can realize the immense amount of work involved for the Pope in such detailed and meticulous verification.

26) The doctors had suggested to Pius XII to take his walk *during the period of digestion.* That was why, during the height of summer, the Pope went out into the gardens even before four o'clock in the afternoon. It also explains why he went out for a walk in all weather. He was not deterred by rain, wind, or cold. He used to say that, after seven winters in Berlin, he had grown accustomed to not being afraid of bad weather.

27) *Discorsi* etc., Vol. XX, p. 457.

28) I have always admired in Pius XII the prompt rapidity with which he became recollected in prayer. The stroke of noon would often be heard while he was discussing some matter with me, or while he was affably listening to or telling some anecdote. He would immediately interrupt the conversation, stand up, join his hands, cast down his eyes and begin slowly to recite the " *Angelus Domini* " with a devotion which

was clear evidence of his constant recollection in God; a recollection which the conversation, with all its cordiality, had not interrupted.

29) Certain photographs of Pius XII in prayer are reproduced in the preceding plates.

30) Cardinal Pacelli suffered from a slight stammer, which was audible in private conversation, but disappeared when he spoke in a loud voice. For this reason, when the Cardinal had to address small groups (e.g. the empoyees of the Secretariate of State), he would instinctively raise the tone of his voice: this gave to what he said a note of declamation and solemnity which was incongruous in certain circumstances. When he became Pope, I did not notice the slight stammer any more, except on very rare occasions.

31) Cf. *Discorsi* etc., Vol. XX, p. 395.

32) Pius XII's exactitude and precision were revealed in innumerable ways. Special importance was given, for instance, to the signature of letters, photographs, or documents. He used very fine nibs—the kind which were called " *perry* " when we were school-boys—; the ink had always to be very black. When the paper to be signed was carefully spread out on the desk, the Pope, with a calm and, you might say, attentive gesture, would take in his right hand the pen which was on the table (always, without fail, in the same place); he would look closely at the nib to see whether some tiny fibre

had found its way in, or some other slight impurity which would have made his handwriting too thick. If he noticed something of the sort or suspected its presence, he would take a small piece of black material (also always on his table and always in the same place) and would carefully clean the nib. Having ascertained that everything was in order, he would put the pen down—this time, next to the paper—pull up, with an unhurried gesture, the right sleeve of his white cassock and grasp the pen between the thumb, index, and middle finger of his right hand, while—stretching out his arm—he raised the tiny lid of the ink-pot with the other fingers. The ink-pot was of a rather old-fashioned type, and the lid was always closed to keep out the dust. The Pope would then immediately dip the nib into the ink, being very cautious not to let it be too full and blot the table or the paper. Finally, the Holy Father came to the act of signing. He wrote very quietly and rather slowly, paying great attention to the light and heavy strokes. He concluded his signature with a rather long " *flourish* " which put the final touch to his finished workmanship. Then he carefully dried the nib with the usual piece of black tissue and made sure that the ink was completely removed (" otherwise "—he would say—" the nib gets rusty and is of no use any more "). He then replaced the scrap of material and the pen. Finally, he handed the signed document to the person present, with repeated recommendations to wait for a while before placing it among other papers, so that the signature—which was too fresh—would not be blotted.

143

It is worth noting that Pius XII's handwriting remained very firm right up to the last days of his life. To be convinced of it, we need only compare the two facsimiles reproduced here: one is from March, 1939, the other from June, 1958.

It was otherwise with Pius XI. During the last years, his handwriting became rather shaky. We reproduce here two of his signatures: one from 1922, the other from 1938.

I recall another incident which shows how precise Pius XII was. In 1937, Pius XI was already ill. Cardinal Pacelli took his regular holidays in Switzerland during the month of October. Every day he called me by telephone. I had drawn up for our conversations a kind of code in which a special meaning was given to common, everyday phrases.

I had made two copies of this curious code: one I kept myself, and the other I gave to the Cardinal who took it with him.

The day after his arrival in Switzerland, there was the first phone call. His Eminence at once asked me: *" Is it raining? "* And I promptly replied: *" Imagine! It's a glorious day!"*

I immediately heard His Eminence saying, almost in a whisper: *" Haven't you got the paper? "* I at once realized my blunder, picked up the sheet on which the code was written, and replied: *" It's still cloudy! "* The person appointed by the Fascist Government to censor our conversations must surely have been amazed at my unexpected rectification ... of the weather bulletin. The fact was that *" Is it raining? "* meant in our code language: *" How is the Pope? "* and *" It's still cloudy "* meant: *" He is still the same."* However, whereas the Cardinal, with his unfailing precision, had begun the conversation with the famous sheet of paper in front of him, I had completely forgotten to use the code.

33) This occurred not only for Italian, but also for foreign languages. I met with a typical instance in December 1954. The Pope was very ill. I was making my report, at his bedside, about the appointment for the diocese of Rodez. I pronounced *" Rodés "*, i.e. with a close *e*. His Holiness in-

terrupted me: "*You know, Monsignor, it is not pronounced 'Rodés', but 'Rodès'*" (with an open *e*). At the moment, partly because I was anxious to finish quickly, partly because I was worried about the Pope's serious state of health, partly from distraction, I continued, in what I was saying, to pronounce "*Rodés*". Pius XII said nothing more. He dismissed me, as usual, with great cordiality. Two days later, I went for another audience and, with some surprise, I saw *three or four tomes* on the Holy Father's bed. He greeted me with a smile and immediately said: "*Now, my dear Monsignor, you know French well...*" Interrupting him, I confessed that unfortunately I do not deserve such praise, adding that I am rather like the good Roman who, when asked if he spoke French, answered: "*Je m'arrange.*" The Pope smiled again and went on: "*You see, the other day I told you that Rodez is pronounced Rodès. But you went on saying Rodés... Rest assured that it is an exception. I have here the best French dictionaries, and they make a note of it.*" And, as he spoke, he wanted me to come closer to his bed so that I could see the dictionaries. There was nothing left for me but to apologize for my ignorance and my inattention.

34) Cf. *Discorsi* etc., Vol. X, p. 192. It is interesting to note here the reference to Mazzini's works, as discovered by the Pope: "*Scritti di G. Mazzini*, Ediz. Nazion. Vol. 39, p. 238, and *passim* in vol. 39 and. vol. 3."

It should be noted finally that, not content with verifying

personally each and every one of the quotations he made in his writings, Pius XII used to entrust a last and final revision to Abbot Albareda, Prefect of the Vatican Library.

A further proof of Pius XII's exactitude in making quotations is to be found even in his testament.

This begins, indeed, with the words " *Miserere mei, Deus, secundum (magnam) misericordiam tuam.*" Some have wondered at the " *magnam* " placed between *brackets*.

There is a minor drama at the back of this. When Pius XII was asked on March 2nd, 1939, whether he accepted the Papacy, he replied in the words of the Psalmist: " *Miserere mei Deus secundum magnam misericordiam tuam.*"

But, in the new Psalter, prepared by his order and published in 1945, the " *magnam* " was deleted. The Holy Father wrote his testament in January, 1956. Whence the minor drama. The Pope was *quoting* the words he had said in 1939; among them was the " *magnam* " which, in 1956, had already been eliminated for some time.

I can imagine that Pius XII must have given some little thought to solving the problem. The solution was to place the " *magnam* " between brackets, in order, on the one hand to safeguard historical accuracy, and on the other not to give the impression that he should be the one to ignore the new version.

35) This was the despair of the journalists. They made regular protests about not being able to know the text of the

148

Pope's speech until the "final" proofs of *L'Osservatore Romano* were ready.

At times there were tragedies. The editors of the most important newspapers and the best known agencies harassed their correspondents with requests and reproaches. The correspondents naturally threw the blame on us, on the proverbial slowness of Rome and the chronic disorganization of the Secretariate of State. But how could we help it? It would have been too easy for the journalists to notice one or another change made in the text at the last moment and even easier to discover the hidden motives underlying it, especially when ... there were none.

The tragic affair occurred especially with the discourse of December 24th, because it was not possible to publish the papal message during the Christmas holidays. For this reason Pius XII decided to advance the date of the presentation of the Christmas wishes. And so the Pope's message was broadcast on December 23rd in 1956 and on the 22nd in 1957.

36) On one occasion we were studying a question he had already handled when he was Nuncio in Germany and which, after many years, was again of immediate importance. After we had searched the files in vain for the report he had sent in at that time, the Holy Father told me exactly the year and the month of the report, adding: " *The subject is treated on page four. I can still see it!* " We found the document and what we were looking for was exactly on page four. Pius XII

also had an amazing memory for faces. He often recognized visitors when they came back for an audience after some years. Once he was receiving a group of American Congressmen. They had scarcely entered his library (there were about twenty of them) when he said to one of their number: " *You came here once before.*" It was true.

37) The following is the list of the addresses and broadcasts given by Pius XII during the last month of his life (September and October 1958):

In *September*:

5th September: To the participants of the VIIth Congress of the "International Society of Blood Transfusion."

7th September: To the participants of the VIIth International Congress of Classical Archaeology.

8th September: To the participants of the IIIrd International Congress of Law Officers.

9th September: To those taking part in the Ist General Assembly of the "Collegium Internationale Neuro-Psycho-Pharmacologicum."

11th September: To the Management and Staff of the "Instituto Nacional Epañol de Previsión."

12th September: To the participants of the VIIth Congress of the "International Society of Hematology."

14th September: To the delegates attending the IIIrd Assembly of the " International Catholic Education Office."

17th September: Broadcast Message to the Xth International Marian Congress in Lourdes.

21st September: To the delegates attending the XIIth International Congress of Philosophy.

22nd September: To the participants of the XVIIth International Congress of Apiculturists.

23rd September: To the Rectors of the Major Seminaries of Latin America.

28th September: To the participants of the VIIth International Congress of the Gas Industry.

28th September: Broadcast Message to the IIIrd National Eucharistic Congress of Ecuador.

In *October*:

2nd October: To the participants of the Congress of Concessionaires of Station Bookstalls.

3rd October: To a pilgrimage of the faithful from North America.

4th October: To the participants of the Xth National Congress of the " Italian Society for Plastic Surgery."

5th October: To the participants of the Vth International Congress of Latin Notaries.

38) It sometimes happened that non-Catholics felt impelled to be converted as a direct result of their audience with the

Holy Father. Father Charles-Roux has informed me of four such cases, giving the full names of the persons concerned.

39) *Judith, 16, 16-19.*

40) Pius XI's sturdy thumps upon the desk in the moments of his righteous and holy indignation will remain famous. In 1936, he made a rather strong speech to a large group of Spaniards—mainly priests and nuns—who had fled before the communist persecution. When he had returned to his study, he asked me: *" Do you think they will reply? "* *" Maybe! "* I answered. And the Pope answered, promptly and resolutely, his fist beating ... the table: *" Then We shall reply too! "*

After the Munich agreements of September 1938, Pius XI would say, referring to the English and French: *" This is not a capitulation, it's a somersault* (' capitombolo ')! *"*

Once—I do not remember very well for what reason—he gave me a solemn scolding. He very quickly calmed down and said: *" Now I feel better! "* I ventured to reply: *" I am the one, Your Holiness, who does not feel better! "* And the Pope, continuing the conversation, found a pretext for making me a present of a watch, which I still have in my possession.

That expression: *" Now I feel better! "* is connected with old memories which Pius XI loved to recall. When he was professor at the Seminary of Milan, he used to take his meals with the other members of the teaching staff. Among them there was one (he would say even the name, but I do not

152

remember it) who thought that, in order to stimulate—for digestion—the secretion of the bile, he needed to get into a good rage. What did he do? At the end of the meal, he would raise with his colleagues some rather difficult question. Naturally, opinions differed. The discussion became heated, and the one who had provoked it did all he could to make it still more sharp and stormy. At a certain moment, however, while the others were still warmed up to their subject, that singular individual would announce with great satisfaction: *" That's enough now! I have digested and I feel fine! "* And he would not say another word.

It must not be thought, however, that Pius XI was gruff and bad-tempered. On the contrary, he too, was mild, kindly, and warm-hearted. His conversation was delightful. He still retained the likings and preferences of a librarian. When he received an interesting book, he was happy. And he received many. As substitute in the Secretariate of State, I was responsible for drafting the letters of thanks. But the Pope was not willing to give me the books. I had to copy exactly the frontispiece of each publication on a separate sheet of paper. Pius XI took the opportunity to explain to me the contents of the book, its importance, and the merits of its author. He knew personally many good authors, and he would recall where and for what reason he had met them the first time (at the Ambrosian or the Vatican Library), the relations he had maintained with them, the other works they had published, the specific field of their competence. Altogether it was a true and proper lesson in culture and bibliography. I remember that, on Easter Sunday, 1936, since no Audiences, were due, he made me come at 9 o'clock and continued until noon, showing me books he had received and giving me all possible details for appropriate letters of thanks.

As a good Milanese, Pius XI had a keen sense of humour. In November, 1936, after the first attack of the serious malady which was to bring him to the grave in little more than two years, the Pope saw no less than five doctors in attendance, among them Father Gemelli. Turning to him, the Holy Father said laughingly: *"Five! Isn't one doctor enough to send a person to the other world?"*

Pius XI had very delicate feelings and gestures. For instance, he used to keep carefully all the presents received during audiences. Almost always they were only insignificant objects. The many newly-married couples—whom he used to receive almost every day—would give him the little boxes containing the traditional sugared almonds. The latter were placed in a large box in the Pope's dining-room. When the box was full, Pius XI would send the sweets to the sick children at the hospital of the " Child Jesus." The little containers, even the simplest and poorest, would be placed—with all the other gifts—in the big cupboards with glass doors which almost covered the walls of the reception-room in his private apartment. From time to time, the Pope would take a walk through

154

the room, stopping in front of the cupboards to look with interest at the large collection of heterogeneous objects. He was happy, as though recalling persons and happenings and living the past over again.

One day, a little boy—having nothing else to give—offered the Holy Father a puppet. Pius XI was delighted, and for several days he kept the toy well in view on his desk and told his visitors about the amusing incident.

Pius XI often recalled his mother with great affection. He would repeat laughingly what his mother used to say to him when he was a boy: "*For right thinking, there's good doctrine; but for wrong thinking, there's only guess-work.*"

The Pope had a wonderfully deep sense of responsibility. When he had made a decision, you could be sure that he would not turn back. He would not even allow the slightest discussion once he had consciously and deliberately decided anything. When Mr. Beck, the Polish Foreign Minister, came to Rome, Pius XI refused to receive him because of his irregular matrimonial situation. His attention was drawn to the fact that, after all, the audience would not have been granted to the person, but to the *Foreign Minister* of a Catholic nation; that the Holy See had diplomatic relations with the state in question; that everyone would have readily understood the serious reasons for not refusing the audience. All in vain. As soon as any one of us entered the Pope's study during those days, he would hear a categorical: "*Don't come and*

talk to me about Mr. Beck's audience! " Even Father Ledo-
chowski, the General of the Jesuits, who was a Pole, tried to
placate the Pope. But without success. He had no sooner
timidly broached the subject than Pius XI, in spite of all his
esteem and affection for the eminent religious, cut him short.

Pius XI was a man of great faith and piety. I can never
forget the day (in January, 1939) when, at the end of an
audience in which he had decided some important matters,
I saw him rest his elbows on the desk and almost hide his
head in his hands while he said: " *Tell me, Monsignor, have
We done all We should have done?*" When I tried to set his
mind at rest, he replied: " *We are about to appear at the judg-
ment-seat of God!* "

In December, 1936, when Pius XI was seriously ill, I did
not see him—I was Substitute in the Secretariate of State—for
more than three weeks. He sent for me on Christmas Eve.
Coming close to his bed, I asked him: " *How are you, Your
Holiness?* " He raised his eyes to heaven and replied very
calmly, almost syllable by syllable: " *I am as God wants me to
be, and so I cannot be anything but well.*" Like a good
Manzonian, the Pope had paraphrased more or less Fra Cri-
stoforo's reply: " *As God wills and as, by His grace, I also
will.*" In one form or another, this is the synthesis of holiness.

I should like to recall here how Pius XI, in 1938, cut short
Cardinal Pacelli' last vacation. It was the end of October, and
His Eminence would have wished to stay in Switzerland until

November 2nd. I had been instructed to speak about the matter to the Holy Father—who was still at Castelgandolfo—and I took the liberty of stressing the point that it would have been good for the Cardinal Secretary of State—after a year of such strenuous work—to rest a little longer, even if it was only for a few days. Pius XI listened to me most kindly. Then he said: *" His Eminence the Secretary of State may do as he pleases. But let him know that We shall return to Rome for the feast of Christ the King "* (i.e. the last Sunday of October), *" and it would be good for His Eminence to return also. You can even tell him,"* he added, *" that, if he comes, We shall receive him at 10 o'clock."* I telephoned the Pope's wishes to Cardinal Pacelli in Switzerland. His Eminence arrived in Rome on Sunday, 30th, at 7 a.m. and, at 10 o'clock, was already in audience.

The real reason for bringing the Secretary of State back earlier was actually the *vulnus* inflicted on the Italian Concordat by Mussolini with the law relating to the Jews. The Pope wanted to discuss it with Cardinal Pacelli and ask his opinion, as he did during that audience.

41) The Pope was very careful to avoid in his conversations any statement which might have the semblance of a lie. This got him into difficulties at times—when he was Secretary of State—in dealing with the diplomats. The latter noticed that, when certain questions were asked, His Eminence did

not give—as was usual with him—a ready and clear reply, but appeared hesitant, as though he were at pains to find a way out of the situation. Once, for instance, His Exc. Pignatti, then Ambassador for Italy, came to me and said: *"There is going to be a consistory very shortly."* I was taken aback, and answered with a laugh: *"Whoever told you?"* The diplomat replied: *"The Cardinal Secretary of State."* When I made a sign of astonishment, he went on: *"It's not that he actually told me; but it was quite clear. On several other occasions, I had asked His Eminence if there would be a consistory. He had always answered: No. But, the other day, when I asked the same question, he answered: 'I don't know.' And,"* concluded the Ambassador, *"since the Cardinal never tells a lie, I understood that this time he did not want to say: No. And so there will be a Consistory."* It was true.

42) The intention here is merely to point out the indiscreetness with which pressure was sometimes brought to bear. It is obvious that, on concrete matters, opinions may be different, and even discordant. This comes either from the difficulty and complexity of certain questions, which have repercussions and, you might say, reach out into many fields, or from the diversity of the persons expressing their opinion. Even when these persons are honest, cultured, upright, and disinterested, they still each have a particular *forma mentis*, the result of study, environment, experience, and personal reflection, as well

158

as of their own temperament and character. One will be inclined to overestimate certain aspects; another will put less emphasis on these and more elsewhere. Some will be prone to intransigence and severity: others lean rather towards half measures and compromise. The former, once they have chosen a course, are not dismayed by the serious consequences it may involve; the latter, to avoid such consequences, would prefer to try a different path. In short, there are the optimists and the pessimists, the hesitant and the resolute, the impulsive and the reflective, the temporizers and those who are always in a hurry. All of that is human, as it is human for a mild and rather timid person to be inclined to seek moral support and a feeling of greater security in his final decision by consulting others, or at least listening to their opinions. And then, just think of a delicate and upright conscience such as that of Pius XII. He wanted to know and sought the opinions of other men to set his own doubts at rest and calm his anxiety of spirit. All of this, however, was merely a condition and, so to speak, the raw material for an intense effort of deep personal reflection and, as it were, of maturation, leading—after the inevitable vacillations—to a final decision that was clear, firm, and carefully weighed. At times the decision would be courageous, and even daring: in certain cases, Pius XII—unlike his predecessors, Benedict XV and Pius XI— even went so far as to modify decisions wich had been un- animously adopted by the Cardinals of one or another Roman

Congregation. Not that he scorned such decisions; but he would study and weigh them carefully and, if he thought fit, modify them or even change them radically. Under these circumstances, if the Pope was disturbed by insistent requests and external pressure during this personal work of meditation, study, and prayer, it was only natural that it should be a cause of suffering to him, especially since it increased the struggle within him between his fear of displeasing others and the fear of making a decision against his will. When a judgment about *persons* was involved, things were even more difficult. Caught between eulogies and criticisms, between praise and blame, favourable and unfavourable opinions, it was impossible for the Pope personally to verify merits and defects, and so he could not bring himself to make the appointments.

43) At times there were curious misunderstandings. Once, for instance, the Pope, speaking of a papal representative from abroad, said to me: " *I received him yesterday, and I warned him—you know about what. I spoke clearly!* " Afterwards, the prelate in question came to see me. He was completely satisfied about his audience with the Holy Father. " *He was so kind, so nice!* " he said. " *He told me repeatedly that he follows my work and thinks very highly of it.* " I broke in at this point: " *But the Holy Father told me that he had warned you ...* " (and I mentioned the subject of the papal admonition). The worthy prelate, quite unruffled, promptly

replied: " *Yes, but he just barely mentioned it, and with such delicacy ... I am really happy, because the Pope is pleased with me!* "

44) Whenever Pius XII had to receive a group of priests, he would seem rather worried. Very often he would say to me (at 9.30 a.m., at least two hours before the scheduled audience): " *Today I shall be receiving a group of priests. Who knows how many requests they will have to make!* " I would smile and say: " *Say no to them all, Your Holiness!* " And the Pope would reply: *Yes, I say no. But then, they insist, they insist ...*" And he would throw up his hands, as if in resignation.

His Predecessor, Pius XI, when he was asked by clerics during audiences for dispensations, privileges, ets., would give a definitely negative answer, which left them with no slightest desire to insist and discouraged anyone else who might have intended making a request. When I was General Chaplain of the Italian Catholic Youth, I once accompanied a group of boys for an audience. With them, there was also a worthy seminarian (today an Archbishop!) who had the enviable ... defect of being too young, and so could not yet be ordained a priest. The lad asked me: " *May I ask the Pope to give me a dispensation for my age?* " " *Try!* " I said. And the seminarian, his voice trembling with emotion and hope, presented his case to the Pope. Pius XI listened to him most kindly and, when he had finished, said: " *You want a dispensation*

161

for your age? " " *Yes* ", replied the seminarian, now almost certain of victory. But the Holy Father calmly went on: " *All right. But ... there is no need for the Pope to intervene. You have only to wait!...* "

45) It is now general knowledge (because Pius XII himself chose to say it publicly) that, in 1952, Mgr. Montini and yours truly asked the Pope to be dispensed from accepting the Cardinalate. This started quite a lot of gossip. Some said that Pius XII had only made the offer *pro forma*, without insisting; others supposed that we had preferred not to leave the Pope, but to remain with him, even without the red zucchetto. The truth is that Pius XII was, as ever, kind and sincere. He not only made the offer, but insisted—for some months!—on his kindly proposal. Finally, he yielded, paternally, to our wish. His intention had been to leave us at our posts, as before. " *No change,*" he would say, " *the only addition will be the red zucchetto!* " And he would laugh heartily when he heard us reply that we were perfectly content to *remain as before,* but ... without the red zucchetto. The Pope used to add that he would have found a title for us, once we were raised to the purple: " *For instance* ", he would say, " *Msgr. Montini, ' Preposto ' for Ordinary Affairs, and Msgr. Tardini, ' Preposto ' for Extraordinary Affairs.*" He was not yet thinking of giving us the title " Pro-Secretary of State." This was conferred on us by the Holy Father after he had already granted our request. I shall always remember how kindly the

Pope said to me one morning, in November, 1952, while he was still at Castelgandolfo: *" But at least you will accept the title of Pro-Secretaries of State?"* I immediately accepted and thanked him. When the news was published, I once again expressed my gratitude to His Holiness. The Pope replied affably: *" My dear Monsignor, you thank me now that you haven't let me do what I wanted? "* I replied: *" Yes, Your Holiness, I am thanking you for what you have done, but much more for what you have not done."* The Pope smiled.

46) *Ep. ad Rom. 7, 15.*

47) *Discorsi* etc., Vol. X, p. 116.

48) Take good note. We say *" outward responsibility "* because—obviously—the Pope cannot yield to anyone else the *" inward responsibility "* for his lofty ministry. It is customary, however, for Popes to have a Cardinal Secretary of State who can publicly represent and, in certain circumstances, even cover the august person of the Roman Pontiff. Pius XII, educated at the school of Cardinals Rampolla, Merry del Val, and Gasparri, was not unaware of this. And yet he chose, even *outwardly,* to expose himself personally, and in actual fact, he was often the target for criticism, accusations, complaints, calumnies. He fully realized what would happen and, when it did happen, he suffered. But he deemed it preferable to show the whole world that the Pope did not shun fatigue and did not hesitate to take upon himself completely all

responsibility for the supreme government of the Church. His intelligence, ability, and almost unlimited capacity for work made even this experiment possible.

49) *Discorsi* etc., Vol. I, p. 438.

50) On March 13th, 1939, Hitler agreed to " *protect Slovak independence.*" Two days later, the Führer also took " *the Czech people under the protection of the German Reich.*" At a distance of more than twenty years, it is interesting to re-read the famous press release of March 15th, 1939:

" The Führer and Chancellor, in the presence of the Foreign Minister von Ribbentrop, received today in Berlin the President of the Czechoslovak Republic, Dr. Hacha and the Czechoslovak Foreign Minister, Dr. Chvalkovski, at the latters' express desire. In the course of the meeting, the grave situation which has developed through the happenings of the last weeks in Czechoslovakia was discussed and examined with complete frankness. On both sides, by common agreement, the conviction was expressed that all efforts should be directed towards ensuring tranquillity, order, and peace in this part of Central Europe. The Czechoslovak President declared that, to further these ends and achieve final pacification, he confidently entrusted to the Führer of the German Reich the destinies of the Czech people and nation. The Führer accepted this declaration and expressed his determination to take the Czech people under the protection of the German Reich and to grant it an autonomous development corresponding to its race."

51) We reproduce here the facsimile of the audience sheet of March 11th, 1940.

ANTICAMERA PONTIFICIA

Si presenteranno all'Udienza di SUA SANTITÀ

LUNEDI' 11 MARZO 1940

ORE 11   S.E.il Ministro degli Affari Esteri di Germania

S.E.Mons. Tardini, Segretario della S.C.per gli AA.EE.SS.

52) While the Nazi troops were in Rome, many soldiers, on their own initiative, attended the general audiences. The Pope, faithful to his purpose of opening to all the doors of

165

their Father's house, made no objection. Nor was that all. Some of those lads approached the Holy Father and spoke to him. At times, real and serious matters of conscience were directly presented to His Holiness. The Pope answered everyone with kindness and courtesy and gave spiritual counsel. He would speak with each one in perfect German and easily recognized, by their accent, those coming from the different parts of Germany. The soldiers went out from the audience happy and wrote to their families, often telling them what the Pope had said and adding that, contrary to the propaganda spread in Germany, Pius XII was very nice and very kind also to Germans. The military censors read these letters and the authorities of the Nazi army became worried. And so the German soldiers were *forbidden* to come to the Vatican.

53) *Discorsi* etc., Vol. XIII, p. 471.

54) *Discorsi* etc., Vol. XIV, p. 429.

55) *Discorsi* etc., Vol. XIII, p. 472.

56) *Discorsi* etc., Vol. XVI, p. 335.

57) *Discorsi* etc., Vol. XIII, p. 433.

58) *Discorsi* etc., Vol. XV, p. 530.

59) *Discorsi* etc., Vol. V, p. 163.

60) *Discorsi* etc., Vol. XIII, p. 429.

61) *Discorsi* etc., Vol. V. pp. 154-155.

62) *Discorsi* etc., Vol. XVIII, pp. 624-625.

63) *Discorsi* etc., Vol. XIII, p. 429.

64) *Discorsi* etc., Vol. XII, p. 384.

65) *Discorsi* etc., Vol. XII, p. 8.

66) *Discorsi* etc., Vol. XVI, p. 340.

67) *Discorsi* etc., Vol. XVI, p. 341.

68) *Discorsi* etc., Vol. XIII, p. 431.

69) *Discorsi* etc., Vol. IX, p. 394.

70) *Discorsi* etc., Vol. XVI, p. 333.

71) *Discorsi* etc., Vol. VIII, p. 351.

72) *Discorsi* etc., Vol. XVIII, p. 737.

73) *Discorsi* etc., Vol. VII, p. 315.

74) *Discorsi* etc., Vol. XV, p. 529.

75) *Discorsi* etc., Vol. XV, p. 530.

76) *Discorsi* etc., Vol. V, p. 122. These words are taken from Pius XII's broadcast on the occasion of the 4th anniversary of the outbreak of the world war. The document was rather short, but of great importance, an importance which escaped many at the time. The Pope's intention was, indeed, to express his disagreement with the formula of " *uncondit-ional surrender* " which had been launched by the Allies after the meeting in Casablanca in January, 1943, and repeated in a thousand ways in the political assemblies, on the radio, and in the press. I quote here the main point of the papal message, which, at a distance of 16 years, will be clearer: " We appeal to all those who bear the responsibility of promoting contact and harmony in the cause of peace and, with prayer welling up from the depths of Our sorrowful heart, We say to them: true strength need not fear to be generous...

" Do not trouble nor dim the peoples' longing desire for peace by acts which, instead of encouraging confidence, rekindle hatred and strengthen the will to resistance.

" Give all nations the well-founded hope of a worthy peace, which shall not offend either their right to live or their sense of honour.

" Make clear beyond all possible doubt that there is honest agreement between your principles and your purposes,

168

On September 30th, 1958, His Holiness Pius XII received the boys from Villa Nazareth for their usual summer audience. The two photographs published here are the last which show the Pope smiling. He was not feeling well, but he did not want the little chaps to give up seeing him. He stayed with them nearly half an hour, always serene, calm, and smiling. He personally distributed candy to the children.

At the end of the audience, Pius XII greeted Msgr. Tardini, who did not think at the time that the affectionate handclasp would count as a last farewell.

between your declarations in favour of a just peace and your actual deeds.

" Only in this way will it be possible to create a serene atmosphere so that the peoples which, at a given moment, are less favoured by the fortunes of war may believe in the revival and growth of a new sense of justice and community between nations and, as a natural result, look towards the future with greater confidence, without having to fear that they may compromise the safety, integrity, and honour of their country " (l. c. pp. 120-121).

Pius XII did not think the formula of " *unconditional surrender* " a happy one; it was too blunt in itself, and he considered it to be in conflict with the programme he had drawn up.

The Pope had, indeed, three aims during the world war:

1. *To avoid anything which might stir up greater bitterness.* For this reason, he refrained as far as possible from pronouncing public and solemn condemnations.

The line he took was excellently described in the Christmas Broadcast for 1946: " The Church, which has been sent by the Divine Saviour to all peoples, to lead them to their eternal salvation, has no intention of intervening and taking sides in controversy on purely earthly matters.

" She is a mother. Do not ask a mother to take sides for or against one or another of her children. All must equally find and feel in her that clear-sighted and generous love, that deep and unchanging affection, which gives her loyal sons the strength to walk more steadfastly along the royal road of truth and light, and awakens in the wayward and erring the longing desire to come once more under her maternal guidance " (*Discorsi* etc., Vol. VIII, p. 352).

This did not prevent Pius XII, in diplomatic and secret documents, from reiterating forceful appeals to rulers to avoid cruelty, injustice, indiscriminate slaughter, endeavouring—as far as was in his power—to *humanize the war*. It is well known that the *Notes* sent by the Holy See to the Nazi Government during those sad days were taken into serious consideration even at the famous Nuremburg trials. The formula of " *unconditional surrender*," however, was likely to arouse fears of all kinds of humiliations for the vanquished peoples, and so to rekindle hatred and stir up resentment.

2. *To shorten the war*. All Pius XII's addresses, from 1939 to 1945, are animated by his keen paternal anxiety to achieve this end. But the harsh demand for " unconditional surrender," with its implied threat of a dark and painful future, might have driven the vanquished—especially the vigorous German people—to desperation, thus prolonging their resistance, and so prolonging the war.

3. *To prepare for peace*. How often, in the darkest days of the war, Pius XII suggested and pointed out the ways of peace! And the bare programme of " *unconditional surrender* " seemed to him to be absolutely lacking in any positive contribution to the future peace. He would have preferred the call to surrender to be accompanied by a guarantee that

170

the conquered peoples would receive a treatment, severe perhaps, but in conformity with their human dignity; above all, he would have wished to see at least a first general outline of a well thought-out and concrete "new order," to facilitate future harmony and collaboration between peoples and, by effective measures, to avoid further war.

The ideas expressed by Pius XII on September 1st, 1943, were confirmed and developed in his Christmas Broadcast for the same year (*Discorsi* etc., Vol. V, pp. 163-164).

77) *Discorsi* etc., Vol. XVIII, p. 656.

78) *Discorsi* etc., Vol. III, p. 41. Pius XII's concept of his *ministerium verbi*, his ministry of the word, is clearly expressed in the Allocution to the Sacred College of Christmas Eve, 1944.

" At a time when the lamentation, *Desiit fidelitas inter filios hominum* (Ps. 11, 2), is fulfilled more poignantly and more sorrowfully than ever before;

at a time when errors, spread abroad with a violence, at times open, at times ill-concealed, strive to win control of public opinion and of all key positions;

at a time when the words: liberty, independence, democracy, are used at the service of certain ambitions and certain trends, as no more than a means for relaxing the vigilance of those whose fidelity would never knowingly consent to abandon or endanger the heritage transmitted to them from the whole Christian past;

at a time when the enemy of Christ and of His Church seeks, more skilfully than ever, in the words of the Apostle of the Gentiles, to " pass for an angel of light " (2 *Cor.* 11, 14);

at a time like this, the Church and the Supreme Pastor, who is responsible for Our Lord's inheritance, have more than ever the duty of proclaiming the Truth, of defending It against the wiles of prevailing errors, without human respect and without weakness; they have the duty of opening the eyes of men of good will, and especially of the faithful, to the dangers of certain modern trends, of sharpening their judgment so that they will discern in time the errors disguised as truth, in order that the peoples may not have to learn too late and at their own expense the truth of the Prophet's bitter warning: *Arastis impietatem, iniquitatem messuistis, comedistis frugem mendacii* (Osee 10, 13) " (*Discorsi* etc., Vol. VI, pp. 231-232).

79) " The Pope has the divine promises. In spite of his human frailty, he is invincible and unshakable. Herald of truth and justice, principle of the Church's unity, his voice denounces errors, idolatries, superstitions, condemns iniquity, wins love for charity and virtue.

" Can he then be silent when, in a nation, the churches united to the centre of Christendom, to Rome, are snatched away by violence or trickery; when all the Greek-Catholic bishops are imprisoned because they do not want to apostatize from their faith; when priests and lay people are persecuted and arrested because they refuse to break away from their true Mother Church?

" Can the Pope be silent when parents are deprived of the right to educate their own children by a minority regime which is trying to take them away from Christ?

" Can the Pope be silent when a state exceeds its competence and arrogates the right to suppress dioceses, depose bishops, overthrow ecclesiastical organization and reduce it to a level below the strict minimum necessary for the effective care of souls?

" Can the Pope be silent when things even go so far that a priest is punished with jail for having refused to violate the most sacred and inviolable of secrets, the secret of sacramental confession?

" Is all of that perhaps unwarranted interference with the political powers of the State? Who could honestly make such a statement? " (*Discorsi* etc., Vol. X, pp. 390-391). To gain a fuller insight into Pius XII's thought on the relations between politics and the action of the Church, it will be useful to consult Vol. XIII of the *Discorsi* ets., p. 422 pf.

80) *Discorsi* etc., Vol. VIII, pp. 105-106.

81) Under these circumstances, we had to have recourse to real acrobatic feats in order to escape the Pope's ever watchful eye. One day, for instance, when I was about to leave

his room, Pius XII asked: *" How is it that there are so few matters to report on? "* I was in a cold sweat. Then, referring to the horrible weather conditions—it was teeming with rain—I said: *" It would seem that with this bad weather, the air-mail service has been suspended! "* The Pope did not answer. But, as soon as I had gone out, he told the person attending him about Mgr. Tardini's ... *escape*. Something worse happened to me on another occasion. I had cut the audience as short as possible. But, as I was going out, the Pope called me to his bedside and, fixing a searching eye upon me, asked, almost with severity: *" Monsignor, have you told me everything? "* And he stressed the *" everything."*

It was difficult to reply. After a moment's embarrassment, I put on a casual air again, and said: *" Your Holiness, I have told almost everything."* And I stressed heavily the *" almost."* The Pope smiled, dismissed me and then told the others about my answer.

82) I call *couch* a kind of *sofa* on which, when he was ill, the Pope used to spend some hours of the day.

83) Pius XII, in order to observe perfectly the rules of canon law, never allowed Holy Mass to be said in his bedroom. The Holy Sacrifice was offered in the adjoining study, and the little altar was placed in such a way that, from his bed—when the door was open—the Pope could see the celebrant.

84) More than once, in December, 1954, Pius XII said to me that, if he had been going to remain ill, he would have given up the Papacy. *" I am only staying at my post,"* he would say, *" because the doctors have assured me that I shall get back my former strength."* And for nearly four years more, the Pope was, in fact, able to stand a tremendous volume of work.

85) *Ep. ad Gal.* 2, 19.

This volume is being sold for the benefit of the boys of " Villa Nazareth "
(Via Pineta Sacchetti, 29 - Rome)

Cum adprobatione ecclesiastica